Adoption and (Scotland) Act 2007

The Act and regulations

Fergus Smith and Roy Stewart
with Alistair Stobie

BAAF ADOPTION & FOSTERING

British Association for Adoption & Fostering
(BAAF)
Saffron House
6–10 Kirby Street
London EC1N 8TS
www.baaf.org.uk

Charity registration 275689 (England and Wales) and
SC039337 (Scotland)

British Library Cataloguing in Publication Data
A catalogue record for this book is available
from the British Library

ISBN 978 1 907585 13 5

Project management by Shaila Shah, Director of
Publications, BAAF
Designed by Helen Joubert Designs
Typeset by Avon DataSet Ltd, Bidford on Avon
Printed in Great Britain by The Lavenham Press
Trade distribution by Turnaround Publisher
Services, Unit 3, Olympia Trading Estate,
Coburg Road, London N22 6TZ

BAAF is the leading UK-wide membership
organisation for all those concerned with
adoption, fostering and child care issues.

Contents

Contents

Contents

*All references in brackets are to the Adoption and Children (Scotland) Act 2007
(AC(S)A 2007) unless otherwise stated.*
CA 1989 = Children Act 1989

Notes about the authors

Fergus Smith is the Director of Children Act Enterprises Ltd (www.caeuk.org), an independent social work consultancy which undertakes research, consultancy, training and independent investigation. Fergus is also the author of over a dozen pocket-sized guides to family and criminal law written in consultation with acknowledged experts in their field.

Roy Stewart is an independent child care consultant and trainer, an independent chair of adoption and fostering panels, and Associate Consultant with Children Act Enterprises. Roy has extensive experience as a practitioner and manager in local authority adoption and fostering services.

Alistair Stobie is a solicitor in Scotland, practising in the public sector with a particular emphasis on permanence planning for "looked after" children. He is also a part-time lecturer in child welfare and protection.

Part A

Concepts, principles and primary legislation

Introduction

- This guide is for use by those in Scotland whose work with children and families involves adoption and permanence planning.

- It is intended to provide easy access to and reinforce understanding of the **Adoption and Children (Scotland) Act 2007** (now fully implemented) as well as its associated Regulations.

- **Part A** of the book summarises principles and concepts underpinning, as well as the main provisions of the new law.

- It is laid out in the following order that reflects the order of the Act itself and includes, where required, a brief reference to the relevant Regulations:

  - **Principles and concepts**

  - **Adoption service**

  - **Adoption process**

  - **Status of adopted children**

  - **Adoption support plans**

  - **Registration**

  - **Adoptions with a foreign element**

  - **Permanence orders**

  - **General**

- **Part B** offers a comprehensive summary of relevant regulations. National adoption standards may be found at www.scotland.gov.uk/Publications/2010/06/01094202/1

■ A subject index enables rapid access to specific subjects.

This guide should be used only to supplement, not replace, reference to source material, statutory guidance and competent legal advice.

Principles and concepts

■ The AC(S)A 2007 is founded upon the following overarching principles:

- **paramountcy of the child's welfare** – in all decisions by courts and adoption agencies;

- **a "welfare checklist"** – expanded beyond just the welfare test;

- **avoidance of undue delay** in planning for permanence and adoption when children cannot be cared for by their birth family;

- **child's views** – so far as ascertainable and taking account of the child's age and maturity;

- **minimum intervention** – an order should not be made unless the order will make things better for the child than not doing so.

■ The Act is also conceptually underpinned by its:

- enhancement of permanence options through the introduction of the permanence order which may itself secure a permanent placement or be used as a stepping stone to adoption;

- introduction of the possibility of unmarried couples adopting jointly;

- encouragement of people to adopt and support of adoption placements by obliging local authorities to ensure that support and required financial assistance are available to those affected by adoption;

- acknowledgement of the lifelong impact of adoption on all parties.

The adoption service

Duty of local authority to provide adoption service [s.1]

- Each local authority must:

  - to the extent that it already provides an adoption service in its area, continue to do so; and

  - to the extent that it does not provide such a service in its area, provide such a service there [s.1(1)].

- In this Act, "adoption service" means services designed to meet the needs, in relation to adoption, of persons mentioned in s.1(3), i.e.:

  - children who may be adopted;

  - persons who have been adopted;

  - parents and guardians of children who may be adopted;

  - natural parents of persons who have been adopted;

  - persons who, before the placing of a child for adoption or the adoption of a child treated the child as their child;

  - siblings (whole-blood or half-blood), natural grandparents and former guardians of children who may be adopted or those who have been adopted;

  - persons who may adopt a child;

  - persons who have adopted a child;

  - in relation to those who may or have adopted a child, children of, or children treated as children of, such persons; and

  - any other persons who are affected by the placing, or proposed placing, of a child for adoption, or affected by an adoption [s.1(2); (3)].

- An adoption service includes, in particular, services consisting of or including:

  - arrangements for assessing children who may be adopted;

  - arrangements for assessing prospective adopters;

  - arrangements for placing children for adoption;

  - provision of information about adoption to any of the persons mentioned in s.1(3); and

  - adoption support services [s.1(4)].

- In this Act, "adoption support services" means services consisting of or including the provision of:

  - counselling to any of the persons mentioned in s.1(3);

  - guidance about adoption to such persons;

  - any other assistance in relation to the adoption process that the local authority providing an adoption service in a particular case considers appropriate in the circumstances of that case [s.1(5)].

  Carrying out duties imposed by s.1 [s.2]
- For the purpose of carrying out the duties imposed by s.1(1) efficiently and effectively, a local authority must have regard to:

  - the other services that it provides in its area in carrying out the functions of a local authority under any of the enactments mentioned in s.5(1B) of the Social Work (Scotland) Act 1968 (power of the Scottish Ministers to issue certain directions) including, in particular, those functions in so far as they relate to children; and

  - any registered adoption service provided there [s.2(1)].

- A local authority may carry out the duties imposed by s.1(1) by securing the provision of its adoption service by a registered adoption service [s.2(2)].

■ In s.2, "registered adoption service" means an adoption service provided as mentioned in s.2(11)(b) of the Regulation of Care (Scotland) Act 2001 and registered under Part 1 of that Act.

Adoption service: regulations [s.3]

■ The Scottish Ministers may by regulations amend s.1(4) or (5) by adding further services, modifying the services mentioned in those subsections or make further provision about adoption services.

Local authority plans [s.4]

■ Before the expiry of such period as the Scottish Ministers may direct, each local authority must prepare and publish a plan for the provision of the adoption service which it is required by s.1(1) to continue to provide, or to provide, in its area [s.4(1)].

■ Each local authority:

  • *must* from time to time review the plan published by it under s.4(1); and

  • *may*, having regard to any such review, prepare and publish modifications of the plan, or a plan in substitution for the plan [s.4(2)].

■ In preparing a plan, or carrying out a review, under s.4 a local authority must consult:

  • each Health Board constituted under s.2 of the National Health Service (Scotland) Act 1978 which provides services under that Act in the area of the local authority;

  • such voluntary organisations as appear to the authority to represent the interests of persons who use, or are likely to use, the adoption service in that area;

  • such voluntary organisations as appear to the authority to provide services in that area which, were they to be provided by the authority, might be an adoption service; and

- such other persons as may be prescribed by regulations made by the Scottish Ministers [s.4(3)].

■ A local authority may incorporate a plan published under s.4(1) in any plan published by the authority under s.19(1) of the 1995 Act (local authority plans for services for children) [s.4(4)].

■ When a local authority incorporates a plan as mentioned in s.4(4), it need not separately publish a plan under s.4(1) [s.4(5)].

■ S.4(2) and (5) apply to a plan modified or substituted under s.4(2) as they apply to a plan published under s.4(1) [s.4(6)].

■ The Scottish Ministers may give a local authority directions as to the carrying out of its functions under s.4(2) [s.4(7)].

■ The Scottish Ministers may vary or revoke any direction given under s.4(7) [s.4(8)].

Guidance [s.5]

■ When a local authority is carrying out its function under s.1 to continue to provide, or to provide, an adoption service or to secure the provision of such a service, the local authority must have regard to any guidance given by the Scottish Ministers [s.5(1);(2)].

■ Guidance such as is mentioned in s.5(2) may, in particular, contain provision in relation to:

- how a local authority should assess (or reassess) the needs of a person for adoption support services;

- how the power conferred by s.9(1) (to assess need for adoption support services by person affected by placing / proposed placing of a child for adoption or affected by adoption) should be exercised;

- the classes of person in relation to whom that power should be exercised;

- how responsibility for provision of an adoption service should be transferred from one local authority to another [s.5(3)].

■ The Scottish Ministers may vary or revoke any guidance such as is mentioned in s.5(2) [s.5(3)].

NB The Guidance can be found at www.scotland.gov.uk/Publications/ 2010/06/01094202/1

Assistance in carrying out functions under s.1 and s.4 [s.6]

■ When it appears to a local authority that an appropriate person could assist the authority in carrying out any of its functions under s.1or s.4, it may require the person to assist the authority in the way specified in the requirement [s.6(1)].

■ An appropriate person need not comply with a requirement made by virtue of s.6(1) if:

- it would not be reasonably practicable to do so;

- doing so would be incompatible with the person's functions (statutory or otherwise); or

- when the person is not a natural person, doing so would unduly prejudice the carrying out of such functions [s.6(2)].

■ For the purposes of s.6 a person is "appropriate" if the person is:

- another local authority;

- a Health Board constituted under s.2 National Health Service (Scotland) Act 1978;

- such other person as may be prescribed by regulations made by the Scottish Ministers [s.6(3)].

Meaning of "adoption service" in Regulation of Care (Scotland) Act 2001 [s.7]

- S.2 Regulation of Care (Scotland) Act 2001 (meaning of "care services"), is amended so that s.2(11) and (12) of the 2001 Act will mean that an adoption service is any service which is provided by a:

  - local authority under s.1(1) of the Adoption and Children (Scotland) Act 2007); or

  - person other than a local authority and which consists of, or includes, services mentioned in s.1(4).

- For purposes of the new s.11(b) of the 2001 Act, the:

  - making by a person of arrangements for the adoption of a child by a "relevant person"; or

  - placing by a person of a child for adoption with a relevant person, is *not* an adoption service.

  NB Here, "relevant person" means a parent of the child, any other "relative" (as per s.119(1)) of the child, or where a parent of the child is a member of a "relevant couple" (as per s.29(3), the other member of the couple.

Adoption agencies: regulations about carrying out of functions [s.8]

- The Scottish Ministers may make regulations for any purpose relating to the carrying out of its functions by a registered adoption service [s.8(1)].

- The Scottish Ministers may make regulations with respect to the carrying out by local authorities of their functions in relation to adoption [s.8(2)].

- Regulations under s.8 may in particular make provision for or in connection with:

  - specifying circumstances in which a local authority proposing to make arrangements for the adoption of a child must apply for a permanence order which includes provision granting authority for the child to be adopted;

- requiring such an application to be made within a period specified in the regulations [s.8(3)].

Adoption support services

Assessment of needs for adoption support services [s.9]

- A local authority:

  - *must*, on the request of a person mentioned in s.1(3) (except the one described immediately below) make an assessment of her/his need for adoption support services;

  - *may*, on the request of a person affected by the placing/proposed placing of a child for adoption or affected by adoption, make an assessment of her/his need for adoption support services [s.9(1)].

- When a local authority makes an assessment of the needs of a person for adoption support services under s.9(1), the authority must decide whether the needs of the person call for the provision of such services [s.9(2)].

- A local authority making an assessment of needs under s.9(1) must:

  - do so in such manner as may be prescribed by regulations made by the Scottish Ministers; and

  - have regard to such matters as may be so prescribed [s.9(2)].

  NB The Adoption Support Services and Allowances (Scotland) Regulations 2009 provide further detail in relation to carrying out assessments and making decisions.

Provision of services [s.10]

- On the request of a person mentioned in s.1(3), a local authority must provide information about adoption to the person [s.10(1)].

- On the request of a child who may be adopted, their parent or guardian or a person who may adopt a child, a local authority:

  - *must* provide an adoption service consisting of or including arrangements for assessing children who may be adopted, for assessing prospective adopters and for placing children for adoption to the person; and

  - *may*, without prejudice to s.10(4)(a), provide adoption support services to that person [s.10(2)].

- For the purposes of s.10(2), it is immaterial whether the local authority has made an assessment of the needs of the person for adoption support services [s.10(3)].

- When a local authority decides under s.9(2) that the provision of adoption support services is called for in respect of:

  - a person mentioned in s.1(3) (except one described immediately below) the authority must provide the services to the person;

  - a person affected by the placing/proposed placing of child for adoption or who is affected by adoption, the authority may provide the services to the person [s.10(4)].

Urgent provision [s.11]

- If in the opinion of a local authority a person mentioned in s.1(3) requires adoption support services as a matter of urgency, nothing in s.9 prevents the authority from providing, or arranging for the provision of, those services for the person without first carrying out an assessment under that section of the person's needs for adoption support services [s.11(1)].

- If by virtue of s.11(1) a local authority provides, or arranges for the provision of, adoption support services the authority must, as soon as is reasonably practicable after such provision, make an assessment of the person's needs for adoption support services [s.11(2)].

Power to provide payment to person entitled to adoption support service [s.12]

■ When a local authority has, in respect of a person, an obligation to provide, or secure provision of an adoption support service under Part 1, or has a power so to provide it and determines that it should, then subject to s.12(4), the authority may, after having regard to the matters mentioned in s.12(3) below, provide the person with a payment instead of the service [s.12(1);(2)].

■ The matters to which the local authority must have regard are:

  • the person's eligibility for assistance from any other body;

  • when the person is so eligible, the availability to the person of that assistance at the time when the service might have been provided to the person by the authority;

  • the ability of the authority to provide, or secure the provision of, the service; and

  • the person's need for the service [s.12(3)].

■ A payment under s.12(2) may be made subject to such conditions (including conditions as to repayment) as the authority considers reasonable [s.12(4)].

■ In imposing conditions under s.12(4), the authority must have regard to the person's eligibility for assistance from any other body [s.12(5)].

Regulations [s.13]

■ The Scottish Ministers may by regulations make provision for or in connection with:

  • determining in circumstances specified in the regulations which local authority is, or may become, responsible for the provision of an adoption service, and/or the making of an assessment of adoption support needs;

- determining the time at which, and the circumstances in which, a local authority's duty to provide an adoption service ends;

- specifying the circumstances in which a local authority may continue to provide an adoption service after the above times have passed;

- specifying the arrangements a local authority may make when a person in respect of whom the authority provides, or has a power or a duty to provide, an adoption service moves outwith the authority's area;

- specifying the persons with whom such arrangements may be made;

- assessing the needs for adoption support services of persons who have moved or who intend to move from one local authority area to another, and/or from outwith Scotland to Scotland [s.13(1)];

- the power conferred by s.13(1) may be exercised so as to make different provision for different adoption services [s.13(2)].

NB Sections 45 to 52 are also relevant to adoption support.

The adoption process

PRELIMINARY
Considerations applying to the exercise of powers by court or adoption agency [s.14]

■ Subsections (2) to (4) below apply whenever a court or adoption agency is coming to a decision relating to the adoption of a child [s.14(1)].

■ The court or adoption agency must have regard to all the circumstances of the case [s.14(2)].

■ The court or adoption agency is to regard the need to safeguard and promote the welfare of the child throughout her/his life as the paramount consideration [s.14(3)].

■ The court or adoption agency must, so far as is reasonably practicable, have regard in particular to the:

• value of a stable family unit in the child's development;

• child's ascertainable views regarding the decision (taking account of the child's age and maturity);

• child's religious persuasion, racial origin and cultural and linguistic background;

• likely effect on the child (throughout life) of the making of an adoption order [s.14(4)].

■ Where an adoption agency is placing a child for adoption, it must have regard, so far as reasonably practicable, to the views of the parents, guardians and other relatives of the child [s.14 (5)].

■ In carrying out the duties imposed on it by s.14(2)–(4), an adoption agency must, before making any arrangements for the adoption of a child, consider whether adoption is likely best to meet the needs of the child or whether there is some better practical alternative for her/him [s.14(6)].

■ If an adoption agency concludes that there is such an alternative it must not make arrangements for the adoption of the child [s.14(7)].

■ Without prejudice to the generality of s.14(4)(b), a child aged 12 or over is presumed to be of sufficient age and maturity to form a view for the purposes of that subsection [s.14(8)].

Pre-adoption requirements

Child to live with adopters before adoption order made [s.15]

■ Where the person applying for the adoption order (the "applicant"), or one of the applicants, is a parent, step-parent or relative of the child, or the child was placed with the applicant, or applicants, by an adoption agency, an adoption order may be made in relation to a child if:

- the child is at least 19 weeks old; and

- at all times during the period of 13 weeks immediately preceding the making of the adoption order the child's home was with the applicants [s.15(1);(2);(3)].

■ In all other cases, an adoption order may not be made in relation to the child unless at all times during the period of 12 months immediately preceding the making of the order the child's home was with the applicants [s.15(1);(2);(4)].

The reference to a period of 13 weeks in s.15(3) should be replaced by reference to a period of 6 months in relation to an adoption proposed to be effected by a Convention adoption order, or an adoption of a child habitually resident outside the British Islands which is proposed to be effected by an adoption order other than a Convention adoption order [s.15(5)].

Home visits [s.16]
■ Where a child was placed for adoption with the applicants by an adoption agency, an adoption order may not be made unless the appropriate court is satisfied that:

- sufficient opportunities to see the child with the applicant or, in the case of an application by 2 applicants, both of them together, in the home environment have been given to the agency [s.16(1);(2)].

■ If the child was not placed for adoption with the applicants by an adoption agency, an adoption order may not be made unless the appropriate court is satisfied that sufficient opportunities to see the child with the applicant or, in the case of an application by two applicants, both of them together, in the home environment have been given:

- if the home is in Scotland, to the local authority within whose area the home is situated;

- if the home is outwith Scotland, to any local authority [s.16(4)].

Reports when child placed by agency [s.17]

■ When an application for an adoption order relates to a child placed for adoption by an adoption agency, the agency must:

- submit to the court a report on the suitability of the applicants, and any other matters relevant to the operation of s.14; and

- assist the court in any manner the court directs [s.17(1);(2)].

NB Rule 8(4) of the Sheriff Court Rules 2009 (S.I. 2009/284) sets out the detailed requirements of the Court Report.

Notification to local authority of adoption application [s.18]

■ Where a child was not placed for adoption with the applicants by an adoption agency:

- an adoption order may not be made in relation to the child unless the applicants have, at least 3 months before the date of the order, given notice to the appropriate local authority of their intention to apply for the order [s.18(1);(2)].

In s.18(2), "appropriate local authority" means, where the applicants have their home in Scotland, the local authority within whose area the home is situated and where they have their home outwith Scotland, any local authority [s.18(3)].

Notice under s.18: local authority's duties [s.19]

■ On receipt of a notice under s.18 in respect of a child, the local authority must:

- investigate the matter; and

- submit to the court a report of the investigation [s.19(1);(2)].

■ The local authority must in particular investigate:

- so far as is reasonably practicable, the suitability of the applicants and any other matters relevant to the operation of s.14 in relation to the application;

- whether there has been a contravention of s.75 (restriction on arranging or placing for adoption) in relation to the child; and

- whether there has been a failure to comply with s.76(2) (adoption society not a registered adoption service) in relation to the child [s.19(3)].

NB Rule 8(4) of the Sheriff Court Rules 2009 (S.I. 2009/284) sets out the detailed requirements of the Court Report.

■ If the authority knows that the child is being "looked after" by another local authority, it must, within 7 days, beginning with the day on which it receives the notice, give the other authority a copy of the notice [s.19(4)].

Restrictions on removal of children placed for adoption

Restrictions on removal: child placed for adoption with consent [s.20]

■ When an adoption agency has placed a child for adoption with persons ("prospective adopters"), and each parent or guardian of the child has, in accordance with such provision as may be made by regulations by the Scottish Ministers, consented to the placement (whether or not each parent/guardian knows the identity of the prospective adopters), a parent or guardian of the child must not remove the child from the care of the prospective adopters without leave of the:

- adoption agency; or

- appropriate court [s.20(1);(2)].

- A person who removes a child in contravention of s.20 commits an offence and is liable on summary conviction to imprisonment for a term not exceeding 3 months or a fine not exceeding level 5 on the standard scale or both [s.20(3)].

Restrictions on removal: notice of intention to adopt given [s.21]

- If persons ("prospective adopters") give notice to the appropriate local authority under s.18(2) in relation to a child, and during the period of 5 years immediately preceding the giving of notice, the child's home has been with the prospective adopters, then (unless s.21(3) applies) a person may not remove the child from the care of the prospective adopters during the period beginning with the giving of notice and ending with the relevant act [s.21(1);(2)].

- S.21(3) applies if:

  - the prospective adopters consent to the removal;

  - a court having jurisdiction to make adoption orders grants leave for the removal;

  - the child is arrested; or

  - the removal is authorised by virtue of any enactment [s.21(3)].

- For the purposes of s.21(2) the "relevant act" means:

  - where, before the expiry of the 3 month period (beginning with the day on which the local authority receives the notice), the prospective adopters apply for an adoption order in relation to the child to whom the notice relates, the making of the application for the adoption order;

  - when the prospective adopters do not apply for an adoption order before the expiry of that period, the expiry of that period [s.21(4);(5)].

- If, during the 3 month period, or the period of 28 days beginning with the expiry of the 3 month period, the prospective adopters give a further notice under s.18(2) to a local authority in respect of the same child, s.21(2) does not apply [s.21(6)].

- A person who removes a child in contravention of s.21 commits an offence and is liable on summary conviction to imprisonment for a term not exceeding 3 months or a fine not exceeding level 5 on the standard scale or both [s.21(7)].

Restrictions on removal: application for adoption order pending [s.22]
- When an application for an adoption order in relation to a child has been made to, but not determined by the appropriate court, **and** during the period of 5 years immediately preceding the making of the application, the child's home has been with the persons applying for the order (the "prospective adopters"), then, except where s.22(3) applies, a person may not remove the child from the care of the prospective adopters [s.22(1);(2)].

- S.22(3) applies if the:

  - prospective adopters consent to the removal;

  - court determining the application grants leave for the removal;

  - child is arrested; or

  - removal is authorised by virtue of any enactment [s.22(3)].

- A person who removes a child in contravention of s.22 commits an offence and is liable on summary conviction to imprisonment for a term not exceeding 3 months or a fine not exceeding level 5 on the standard scale or both [s.22(4)].

Restrictions on removal of a child looked after by a local authority [s.23]
- The local authority must not (unless s.23(3) below applies) remove the child from the care of prospective adopters if:

- prospective adopters give notice under s.18(2) in relation to a child, and during the period of 5 years immediately preceding the giving of notice, the child's home has been with the prospective adopters; or

- an application for an adoption order in relation to a child has been made by prospective adopters to, but not determined by the appropriate court, and during the period of 5 years immediately preceding the making of the application, the child's home has been with the persons applying for the order; and

- Before the child's home came to be with the prospective adopters, the child was looked after by a local authority, and continues to be looked after by a local authority [s.23(1);(2)].

■ S.23(3) applies if:

- removal is made in accordance with ss.25 or 26,

- an appropriate court grants leave for the removal,

- removal is authorised by virtue of Chapter 2 or 3 of Part II of the 1995 Act (e.g. an order of a Children's Hearing or emergency protection measures such as a child protection order) [s.23(3)].

Return of children

Return of child removed in breach of certain provisions [s.24]

■ The relevant court may, on the application of a person from whose care a child has been removed in breach of any of the relevant provisions, order the person who has so removed the child to return the child to the applicant [s.24(1)].

■ The relevant court may, on the application of a person who has reasonable grounds for believing that another person is intending to remove a child from the applicant's care in breach of any of the relevant provisions, by order direct that other person not to remove the child from the applicant's care in breach of the provision concerned [s.24(2)].

- The "relevant court" is:

  - if there is pending in respect of the child an application for an adoption order or a permanence order, the court in which the application is pending;

  - in any other case, the Court of Session, or the Sheriff Court of the Sheriffdom within which the applicant resides [s.24(3)].

- The "relevant provisions" are:

  - ss.20, 21, 22 and 23,

  - ss.30, 34, 35 and 36 of the 2002 Act,

  - articles 28 and 29 of the Northern Ireland Order [s.24(4)].

Return of child placed for adoption by an adoption agency [s.25]

- S.25 applies where:

  - in pursuance of arrangements made by an adoption agency or a registered adoption society for the adoption of a child by persons (the "prospective adopters"), the child has been placed with the prospective adopters; and

  - no adoption order has been made in relation to the child on the application of the prospective adopters [s.25(1)].

- The prospective adopters may give notice to the agency or society of their intention not to retain the care of the child [s.25(2)].

- The agency or society may give notice to the prospective adopters of its intention not to allow the child to remain in the care of the prospective adopters [s.25(3)].

- If an application for an adoption order in relation to the child has been made by the prospective adopters, notice under s.25(3) may be given only with leave of the court which is hearing the application [s.25(4)].

- When notice is given by virtue of s.25(2) or (3), or an application for an adoption order made by the prospective adopters is refused or withdrawn, the prospective adopters must, before the expiry of the relevant period, return the child to:

  - the agency or, as the case may be, society; or

  - a person nominated by the agency or, as the case may be, society for the purposes of this section [s.25(5);(6)].

- In s.25(6), "relevant period" means:

  - in the case of notice given under s.25(2) or (3) a period of 7 days beginning with the day on which notice was given;

  - in the case of an application made by prospective adopters which is withdrawn or refused, a period of 7 days beginning with the day on which the application was refused or withdrawn, or longer (maximum 6 weeks) if a court so orders [s.25(7)].

- A person who fails to return a child in contravention of this section commits an offence and is liable on summary conviction to imprisonment for a term not exceeding 3 months or a fine not exceeding level 5 on the standard scale or both [s.25(8)].

- The court by which a person is convicted by virtue of s.25(8) may order that the child in respect of whom the offence is committed be returned to the child's parent or guardian or, as the case may be, the adoption agency or registered adoption society [s.25(9)].

Adoption not proceeding: arrangements

Looked after children: adoption not proceeding [s.26]
- S.26 applies where:

  - prospective adopters give notice under s.18(2) in relation to a child, and

- the child has a home with the prospective adopters, and

- the child was not placed with the prospective adopters in pursuance of arrangements made by an adoption agency or a registered adoption society for the adoption of the child by the prospective adopters, and

- the child is being looked after by a local authority (the "relevant local authority") [s.26(1)].

■ The prospective adopters may give notice to the relevant local authority of their intention not to retain the care of the child [s.26(2)].

■ The authority may give notice to the prospective adopters of its intention not to allow the child to remain in the care of the prospective adopters [s.26(3)].

■ When notice is given by virtue of s.26(2) or (3) the prospective adopters must, before the expiry of the period of 7 days beginning with the day on which notice is given, deliver the child to:

- the authority; or

- a person nominated by the authority for the purposes of s.26 [s.26(4)].

■ If an application for an adoption order in relation to the child has been made by the prospective adopters, notice under s.26(3) may be given only with leave of the court which is hearing the application [s.26(5)].

■ If an application for an adoption order in relation to the child is refused or withdrawn, the child —

- must be delivered to the relevant local authority only if the authority requires it; and

- when such a requirement is made, must be delivered before the expiry of the period of 7 days beginning with the day on which the requirement is made [s.26(6)].

■ When an application by the prospective adopters for an adoption order in relation to the child has been made but not disposed of, any right of the relevant local authority to require the child to be delivered otherwise than by virtue of this section is suspended [s.26(7)].

■ A person who fails to deliver a child in contravention of s.26 commits an offence and is liable on summary conviction to imprisonment for a term not exceeding 3 months or a fine not exceeding level 5 on the standard scale or both [s.26(8)].

■ The court by which a person is convicted by virtue of s.26(8) may order that the child in respect of whom the offence is committed be delivered to the child's parent or guardian or, as the case may be, the relevant local authority [s.26(9)].

In s.26 "registered adoption society" has the meaning given by s.2(2) of the Adoption and Children Act 2002 (England and Wales) [s.26(10)].

Contravention of ss.30–36 of Adoption and Children Act 2002 [s.27]

■ A person who contravenes any of the provisions of the 2002 Act mentioned in s.27(2) commits an offence and is liable on summary conviction to imprisonment for a term not exceeding 3 months or a fine not exceeding level 5 on the standard scale or both.

■ Those provisions are:

   • s.30(1), (2) and (3) (removal of child placed or who may be placed for adoption);

   • s.32(2)(b), 33(2) and 35(2) (return of child by prospective adopters);

   • s.34(1) (removal of child in contravention of placement order);

   • s.36(1) (removal of child in non-agency case);

   • s.36(5) (return of child to parent or guardian) [s.27(2)].

The making of adoption orders

Adoption orders [s.28]

- An adoption order is an order made by the appropriate court on an application under s.29 or s.30 vesting the parental responsibilities and parental rights in relation to a child in the adopters or adopter [s.28(1)].

- The court must not make an adoption order unless it considers that it would be better for the child that the order be made than not [s.28(2)].

- An adoption order may contain such terms and conditions as the court thinks fit [s.28(3)].

- An adoption order may be made in respect of a person aged 18 or over if the application for the order was made when the person was under 18 [s.28(4)].

- An adoption order may be made in respect of a child who is subject to a permanence order [s.28(5)].

- An adoption order may be made even if the child to be adopted is already an adopted child [s.28(6)].

- An adoption order may not be made in respect of a person who is or has been:

  • married, or

  • a civil partner [s.28(7)].

Adoption by certain couples [s.29]

- An adoption order may be made on the application of a relevant couple where:

  • each member is 21 or over;

- neither member is a parent of the child to be adopted; and

- one of the conditions in s.29(2) is met [s.29(1)].

■ Those conditions are that:

- a member of the couple is domiciled in a part of the British Islands;

- each member of the couple has been habitually resident in a part of the British Islands for a period of at least 1 year ending with the date of the application [s.29(2)].

■ A couple is "relevant" for the purposes of s.29 if its members are persons who are:

- married to each other;

- civil partners of each other;

- living together as if husband and wife in an enduring family relationship; or

- living together as if civil partners in an enduring family relationship [s.29(3)].

■ In s.29 "parent" in relation to the child to be adopted, means a parent who has any parental responsibilities or parental rights in relation to the child [s.29(4)].

Adoption by one person [s.30]

■ An adoption order may be made on the application of a person ("A") if:

- A is aged 21 or over;

- s.30(2), (3), (4) or (5) applies;

- one of the conditions in s.30(6) is met; and

- if A is a natural parent of the child to be adopted, s.30(7) applies [s.30(1)].

- S.30(2) applies if A is not a member of a relevant couple [s.30(2)].

- S.30(3) applies if:

  - A and another person ("B") are a relevant couple;

  - B is aged 18 or over;

  - B is a parent of the child to be adopted; and

  - B is domiciled in a part of the British Islands, or has been habitually resident in a part of the British Islands for a period of at least 1 year ending with the date of the application [s.30(3)].

- S.30(4) applies if:

  - A and B are married to or civil partners of each other;

  - B is not a parent of the child to be adopted; and

  - the court is satisfied that B cannot be found; A and B have separated and are living apart and the separation is likely to be permanent; or B is by reason of ill-health (whether physical or mental) incapable of making an application for an adoption order [s.30(4)].

- S.30(5) applies if:

  - A and B are a relevant couple by virtue of being an unmarried couple living together as if husband and wife or as if civil partners in an enduring family relationship as per s.29(3)(c) or (d);

  - B is not a parent of the child to be adopted; and

  - the court is satisfied that B is by reason of ill-health (physical or mental) incapable of making an application for an adoption order [s.30(5)].

- The conditions relevant to s.30(1) are that:

  - A is domiciled in a part of the British Islands;

  - A has been habitually resident in a part of the British Islands for a period of at least 1 year ending with the date of the application [s.30(6)].

- S.30(7) applies if the court is satisfied that:

  - the other natural parent is dead;

  - the other natural parent cannot be found;

  - by virtue of s.28 Human Fertilisation and Embryology Act 1990 (disregarding s.28(5A) to (5I) of that Act), there is no other parent; or

  - the exclusion of the other natural parent from the application for adoption is justified on some other ground [s.30(7)].

  In s.30(3)(c), (4)(b) and (5)(b), the term "parent" has the meaning given by s.29(4), i.e. in relation to a child to be adopted it means a parent who has any parental responsibilities or rights in relation to the child [s.30(8)].

Parental etc consent [s.31]
- An adoption order may not be made unless one of the five conditions is met [s.31(1)].

- The **first** condition is that, in the case of each parent or guardian of the child, the appropriate court is satisfied that:

  - the parent or guardian understands what the effect of making an adoption order would be and consents to the making of the order (whether or not the parent or guardian knows the identity of the persons applying for the order), or

  - the parent's or guardian's consent to the making of the adoption order should be dispensed with on one of the grounds mentioned in s.31(3) [s.31(2)].

- The grounds for dispensing with consent are that:

  - the parent or guardian is dead;

  - the parent or guardian cannot be found or is incapable of giving consent;

- s.31(4) or (5) applies;

- when neither s.31(4) or (5) applies, the welfare of the child otherwise requires the consent to be dispensed with [s.31(3)].

■ S.31(4) applies if the parent or guardian:

- has parental responsibilities or parental rights in relation to the child other than those mentioned in s.1(1)(c) and 2(1)(c) of the Children (Scotland) 1995 Act (i.e. other than the responsibility and right of direct contact);

- is, in the opinion of the court, unable satisfactorily to discharge those responsibilities, or exercise those rights; and

- is likely to continue to be unable to do so [s.31(4)].

■ S.31(5) applies if:

- the parent or guardian has, by virtue of the making of a relevant order (i.e. a permanence order without authority to adopt), no parental responsibilities or parental rights in relation to the child; and

- it is unlikely that such responsibilities will be imposed on, or such rights given to the parent or guardian [s.31(5);(6)].

■ The **second** condition is that a permanence order granting authority for the child to be adopted is in force [s.31(7)].

■ The **third** condition is that each parent or guardian of the child has consented under s.20 Adoption and Children 2002 Act (advance consent to adoption), has not withdrawn the consent and does not oppose the making of the adoption order [s.31(8)].

■ The **fourth** condition is that:

- the child has been placed for adoption by an adoption agency (within the meaning of s.2(1) of the 2002 Act) with the prospective adopters in whose favour the adoption order is proposed to be made;

- the child was placed for adoption under s.19 of the 2002 Act (placing children with parental consent) with the consent of each parent or guardian and the consent of the mother was given when the child was at least 6 weeks old, or under an order made under s.21 of the 2002 Act (placement orders) and the child was at least 6 weeks old when the order was made; and

- no parent or guardian of the child opposes the making of the adoption order [s.31(9)].

■ The **fifth** condition is that an order under Article 17(1) or 18(1) of the Northern Ireland Order (orders declaring children free for adoption) is in force in relation to the child [s.31(10)].

Consent is ineffective for the purposes of s.31(2) if given by the mother fewer than 6 weeks after the child's birth [s.31(11)].

■ A parent or guardian may not oppose the making of an adoption order under s.31(8) or (9) without leave of the court [s.31(12)].

■ The court must not give leave under s.31(12) unless satisfied that there has been a change of circumstances since the consent of the parent or guardian was given or, as the case may be, the order under s.21 Adoption and Children Act 2002 was made [s.31(13)].

■ Its withdrawal is ineffective if consent is given after an application for an adoption order is made:

- to the placement of a child for adoption under s.19, or under an order under s.21 of the 2002 Act; or

- under s.20 of that Act [s.31(14)].

■ In s.31(2) and (3), "parent", in relation to the child to be adopted, means:

- a parent who has any parental responsibilities or parental rights in relation to the child; or

- a parent who, by virtue of a permanence order which does not include provision granting authority for the child to be adopted, has no such responsibilities or rights [s.31(15)].

Consent of child aged 12 or over [s.32]

■ Unless the court is satisfied that the child is incapable of consenting to the order, an adoption order may not be made in respect of a child aged 12 or over unless s/he consents [s.32(1);(2)].

Restrictions on making orders [s.33]

■ Except when s.31(2) applies, the court may not hear an application for an adoption order in relation to a child where a previous application falling within s.33(3) made in relation to the child by the same persons was refused by any court [s.33(1)].

■ S.33(2) applies where:

- in refusing the previous application, the court directed that s.33(2) should not apply; or

- it appears to the court that, because of a change in circumstances, or for any other reason, it is proper to hear the application [s.33(2)].

■ An application falls within s.33(3) if it is an application for an:

- adoption order;

- adoption order as defined in s.46(1) of the Adoption and Children Act 2002;

- order made, or having effect as if made, under Article 12 of the Northern Ireland Order;

- order for adoption made in the Isle of Man;

- order for adoption made in any of the Channel Islands [s.33(3)].

Contravention of s.72 no bar to making order [s.34]

- The court may make an adoption order in relation to a child even where it is found that the applicants have, as respects the child, contravened s.72 (prohibited payments) [s.34)].

Effect of order on existing rights etc [s.35]

- When an adoption order is made on the application of a member of a relevant couple by virtue of s.30(3), the making of the order:

  - does not affect any parental responsibilities and parental rights which immediately before the making of the order were vested in the other member of the relevant couple;

  - does not extinguish any duty owed to the child by that other member to pay or provide aliment in respect of any period occurring after the making of the order, to make any payment arising out of parental responsibilities and parental rights in respect of such a period [s.35(1)].

- Otherwise, the making of an adoption order:

  - extinguishes any parental responsibilities and parental rights relating to the child which immediately before the making of the order were vested in any person;

  - subject to s.35(3), extinguishes any duty owed to the child immediately before the making of the order to pay or provide aliment in respect of any period occurring after the making of the order, to make any payment arising out of parental responsibilities and parental rights in respect of such a period [s.35(2)].

- The making of an adoption order does not extinguish a duty arising under a deed or agreement which:

  - constitutes a trust; or

  - expressly provides that the duty is not to be extinguished by the making of an adoption order [s.35(3)].

- An adoption order does not affect parental responsibilities and parental rights so far as they relate to any period before the making of the order [s.35(4)].

Revocation of supervision requirement [s.36]

- When a child to be adopted is subject to a supervision requirement, and the appropriate court is satisfied that, were it to make an adoption order in relation to her/him, compulsory measures of supervision would no longer be necessary, the court must make an order providing that, on the making of the adoption order, the supervision requirement ceases to have effect [s.36(1);(2)].

Adoption records

Information to be kept about adoptions [s.37]

- The Scottish Ministers may make regulations for or in connection with specifying:

  - information which an adoption agency must keep in relation to adoptions; and

  - form and manner in which it must keep it.

Disclosure of information kept under relevant enactment [s.38]

- The Scottish Ministers may by regulations make provision for or in connection with the disclosure by adoption agencies to adopted persons and other persons of a description or descriptions specified in the regulations of information kept by virtue of a relevant enactment [s.38(1)].

- Regulations under s.38(1) may in particular include provision:

  - in circumstances specified in the regulations, conferring discretion on adoption agencies as to whether to disclose or withhold information;

- specifying conditions which are to apply in relation to the disclosure of information, or information of a type so specified, to adopted persons of a description or descriptions so specified;

- specifying circumstances in which information should not be disclosed to adopted persons of a description or descriptions so specified;

- about the review of decisions of adoption agencies in connection with the disclosure of information, the conditions applicable to such disclosure [s.38(2)].

In s.38 "relevant enactment" means s.37, or any other enactment (whether or not in force) which imposes a requirement (however expressed) to keep records relating to adoptions [s.38(3)]. Relevant data protection amending regulations are still awaited from the Westminster Government.

Status of adopted children

Meaning of adoption [s.39]
- In s.39–s.44, "adoption" means:

- adoption by an adoption order;

- adoption by an adoption order as defined in s.46(1) of the Adoption and Children Act 2002;

- adoption by an order made, or having effect as if made, under Article 12 of the Northern Ireland Order;

- adoption by an order made in the Isle of Man or any of the Channel Islands;

- a Convention adoption;

- an overseas adoption; or

- an adoption recognised by the law of Scotland and effected under the law of any other country [s.39(1)].

Status conferred by adoption [s.40]

■ An adopted person is to be treated in law as if born as the child of the adopters or adopter [s.40(1)].

■ An adopted person is to be treated as the child of the couple concerned if an adopted person is adopted:

• by a relevant couple, or

• by virtue of s.30(3), by a member of a relevant couple [s.40(2)].

■ An adopted person adopted by virtue of s.30(3) by a member of a relevant couple is to be treated in law as not being the child of any person other than the adopter and the other member of the couple [s.40(3)].

■ Otherwise, an adopted person is to be treated in law as not being the child of any person other than the adopters or adopter [s.40(4)].

■ S.40(3) and (4) do not affect any reference in this Act to a person's natural parent or to any other natural relationship [s.40(5)].

■ S.40(7) applies if, in the case of a person adopted under a Convention adoption, the Court of Session is satisfied, on an application under s.40 that:

• under the law of the country in which the adoption was effected the adoption is not a full adoption;

• the consents mentioned in Article 4(c) and (d) of the Convention have not been given for a full adoption, or the UK is not the receiving State (within the meaning of Article 2 of the Convention); and

• it would be more favourable to the person for a direction to be given under s.40(7) [s.40(6)].

■ The court may direct that s.40(4):

• is not to apply; or

- is not to apply to such extent as may be specified in the direction [s.40(7)].

■ In s.40(6), "full adoption" means an adoption by virtue of which the person falls to be treated in law as if the person were not the child of any person other than the adopters or adopter [s.40(8)].

S.40 has effect from the date of the adoption and subject to the provisions of ss.39–44 applies for the interpretation of enactments or instruments passed or made before as well as after the adoption and so applies subject to any contrary indication, and has effect as respects things done, or events occurring, on or after the adoption [s.40(10)].

Miscellaneous enactments [s.41]

■ Subject to s.41(2), s.40 does not apply:

- for the purposes of determining the forbidden degrees of consanguinity and affinity in respect of the law relating to marriage or to the eligibility of persons to register as civil partners of each other, or

- in respect of the crime of incest [s.41(1)].

■ On the making of an adoption order, the adopter and the person adopted are deemed, for all time coming, to be within the forbidden degrees in respect of the law relating to marriage, to such eligibility and to incest [s.41(2)].

■ S.40 does not apply for the purposes of any provision of:

- the British Nationality Act 1981;

- the Immigration Act 1971;

- any instrument having effect under either of those Acts;

- any other law for the time being in force which determines British citizenship, British overseas territories citizenship or British overseas citizenship [s.41(3)].

Pensions [s.42]

- S.40 does not affect entitlement to a pension which is payable to or for the benefit of a person and is in payment at the time of the person's adoption.

Insurance [s.43]

- S.43(2) and (3) apply where a child is adopted whose natural parent has effected for the payment on the death of the child of money for funeral expenses insurance with:

  - a friendly society,

  - a collecting society, or

  - an industrial insurance company [s.43(1)].

- The rights and liabilities under the policy are by virtue of the adoption transferred to the adoptive parents [s.43(2)].

- For the purposes of the enactments relating to such societies and companies, the adoptive parents are to be treated as the person who took out the policy [s.43(3)].

- If the adoption is effected by an order made by virtue of s.30(3), the references in s.43(2) and (3) to the adoptive parents are to be read as references to the adopter and the other member of the relevant couple [s.43(4)].

Succession and "inter vivos" deeds [s.44]

- S.40 does not affect the law relating to adopted persons in respect of:

  - succession to an intestate or testate estate, and

  - disposal of property by virtue of an *inter vivos* deed.

Adoption support plans

Adoption support plans

- S.45 applies when:

  - a local authority has, by virtue of s.9(1), assessed the needs of a person for adoption support services and decides that the provision of such services is called for in respect of the person; and

  - the person is a member of a relevant family [s.45(1)].

- Subject to s.45(4), the authority must prepare an Adoption Support Plan in respect of each member of the relevant family. An Adoption Support Plan must, in relation to the person it concerns ("the person"):

  - specify the needs of the person identified as a result of an assessment carried out by virtue of s.9(1);

  - record details of the adoption support services the provision of which the authority decides is called for by virtue of s.9(2);

  - specify any other needs of the person identified by the authority;

  - set out how the above mentioned needs may be met by the provision of adoption support services;

  - record details of any previous assessment of needs in respect of the person carried out by virtue of s.9(1);

  - record details of any assessment of needs in respect of the person made under s.12A(1) Social Work (Scotland) Act 1968;

  - where the person has been adopted, record details of any care plan prepared by a local authority in respect of the person under regulations made under s.17 Children (Scotland) Act 1995;

  - record details of any adoption support services which were provided to the person before the plan was prepared, or are being provided to the person when the plan is prepared;

- specify any other matter which, in the opinion of the local authority preparing the plan, is relevant to the provision of adoption support services to the person; and

- when there is no information to be included in the plan under any of the above paragraphs record that fact [s.45(2);(3)].

■ The authority may, with the consent of each member of the relevant family aged 12 or over, prepare a single adoption support plan in respect of all members of the relevant family instead of preparing adoption support plans in respect of each of them [s.45(4)].

S.45(5) variously amends the provisions of s.45(3) to reflect the possibility of a single adoption support plan in respect of all members of the relevant family.

■ If in the opinion of the authority a member of the relevant family aged 12 or over is incapable of giving consent under s.45(4), the requirement to obtain such consent does not apply in relation to the member [s.45(6)].

■ In s.45, "relevant family" means:

- a child who is placed for adoption;

- the person or persons with whom a child is placed for adoption;

- a child who has been adopted;

- the person who has, or persons who have, adopted that child;

- any child of the adopters (and any child treated as their child) living in the same household [s.45(7)].

Duration [s.46]
■ An adoption support plan ceases to have effect on the occurrence of whichever of the events in s.46(2) first occurs [s.46(1)].

■ Those events are the:

- preparation of a further adoption support plan in respect of the member or, as the case may be, members of the relevant family in relation to whom the adoption support plan was prepared;

- date on which an appropriate child reaches the age of 18 [s.46(2)].

■ In s.46, "appropriate child" means a child who has been placed for adoption, or who has been adopted and who is a member of the relevant family in relation to which, or to any members of which, the adoption support plan was prepared [s.46(3)].

Family member's right to require review of plan [s.47]

■ S.47 applies where an adoption support plan is in force in respect of a member of a relevant family or, as the case may be, a relevant family [s.47(1)].

■ Subject to s.47(4), the person to whom the plan relates or, as the case may be, a member of the relevant family to which the plan relates (in either case, the "relevant member") may, if the relevant member believes the local authority is not complying with any of its obligations mentioned in the plan, require the authority to review the plan [s.47(2)].

■ The authority may, in reviewing the plan, carry out a reassessment of the needs of the relevant member for adoption support services [s.47(3)].

■ A relevant member (other than the person or persons with whom the child has been placed for adoption or the person who has, or persons who have, adopted the child) may not make a requirement under s.47(2) unless, in the opinion of the local authority, the member is capable of understanding the need for adoption support services [s.47(4)].

■ After reviewing the plan, the local authority must vary the plan to reflect any changes in the:

- needs of any relevant member for adoption support services identified as a result of a reassessment of needs made under s.47(3);

- adoption support services the local authority will provide [s.47(5)].

■ In s.47, any references to a reassessment of needs of a person include, where no assessment has been carried out by virtue of s.9 in relation to the person, references to an assessment of needs of the person [s.47(6)].

Other cases when authority is under duty to review plan [s.48]
■ S.48 applies where an adoption support plan is in force [s.48(1)].

■ The local authority must review the plan:

- from time to time, and

- at any time when the authority becomes aware of a change in the circumstances of a relevant member [s.48(2)].

■ In reviewing the plan, the authority may make a reassessment of the needs of any relevant member [s.48(3)].

■ After reviewing the plan, the authority must vary the plan to reflect any changes in the:

- needs of any relevant member for adoption support services identified as a result of a reassessment of needs made under s.48(3);

- adoption support services the local authority will provide [s.48(4)].

■ In s.48 any references to a reassessment of needs of a person are to be construed in accordance with s.47(6) and "relevant member" has the same meaning as in s.47 [s.48(5)].

Reassessment

Reassessment of needs for adoption support services [s.49]
■ S.49 applies where an adoption support plan is in force [s.49(1)].

- Any relevant member aged 12 or over may require the local authority which prepared the plan to make a reassessment of the member's needs for adoption support services [s.49(2)].

- The authority, having regard to the results of that reassessment, must decide whether the needs of the member call for the provision of such services [s.49(3)].

- If the authority decides, by virtue of s.49(3), that the provision of adoption support services is called for, the authority must provide the services [s.49(4)].

- Where the authority provides adoption support services under s.49(4), it must vary the adoption support plan to reflect any changes in the services the authority will provide [s.49(5)].

- A relevant member (other than the person or persons with whom the child has been placed for adoption or the person who has, or persons who have, adopted the child) may not require a reassessment to be made under s.49 (2) unless, in the opinion of the local authority, the member is capable of understanding the need for adoption support services [s.49(6)].

- Where a local authority is making a reassessment of needs under this section, it must:

  • do so in such manner as may be prescribed by regulations made by the Scottish Ministers; and

  • have regard to such matters as may be so prescribed [s.49(7)].

- In s.49 any references to a reassessment of needs of a person are to be construed in accordance with s.47(6) and "relevant member" has the same meaning as in s.47 [s.49(8)].

Directions

Implementation of plans: directions [s.49]

- The Scottish Ministers may give directions of a general or specific nature to a local authority as to the implementation of adoption support plans [s.50(1)].

- A direction under s.50(1) may not require an authority to provide or, as the case may be, continue to provide, or withhold provision of, a particular adoption support service [s.50(2)].

- The Scottish Ministers may vary or revoke any direction under s.50(1) [s.50(2)].

Guidance and regulations [ss.51; 52]

- In preparing or reviewing adoption support plans, a local authority must have regard to any guidance issued by the Scottish Ministers [s.51(1)].

- The Scottish Ministers may vary or revoke any such guidance [s.51(2)].

- The Scottish Ministers may by regulations make provision for or in connection with specifying the way in which reviews of adoption support plans are to be carried out [s.52].

The Adoption Support Services and Allowances (Scotland) Regulations 2009 and the Guidance issued by the Scottish Government provide further details.

Registration

Adopted children register and index: directions [s.53]

- The Registrar General must continue to maintain:

- a register to be called the Adopted Children Register, and

- an index of the Adopted Children Register [s.53(1)].

■ No entries may be made in the Adopted Children Register other than entries:

- directed to be made in it by adoption orders, or

- required to be made under Schedule 1 [s.53(2)].

■ The provisions of the Registration of Births, Deaths and Marriages (Scotland) Act 1965 with regard to the correction of errors in entries apply in relation to entries in the Adopted Children Register as they apply in relation to entries in any register of births [s.53(3)].

Searches and extracts [s.54]

■ The terms, conditions and regulations as to payment of fees, form and authentication of documents and otherwise applicable under the Registration of Births, Deaths and Marriages (Scotland) Act 1965 in respect of searches in indexes kept by virtue of that Act by the Registrar General, and the supply from the General Register Office of extracts of entries in the registers of births, deaths and marriages, apply in respect of searches in the index of the Adopted Children Register and supplies of extracts of entries in the Adopted Children Register [s.54(1)].

■ When a person makes a request in accordance with those terms, conditions and regulations (including paying such fee as may be prescribed by those regulations), the Registrar General is, if the General Register Office is open for the purpose, to:

- search (or permit the person to search) the index of the Adopted Children Register, and

- issue to the person an extract of an entry in the register [s.54(2)].

Connections between the register and birth records [s.55]

■ The Registrar General must make traceable the connection between any entry in the register of births which, by virtue of para. 2(2) of Schedule 1 or any enactment at the time in force, has been marked "Adopted" and any corresponding entry in the Adopted Children Register [s.55(1)].

■ Information kept by the Registrar General for the purposes of s.55(1) is not to be open to public inspection or search [s.55(2)].

■ The Registrar General may disclose any such information only in accordance with s.55(4) [s.55(3)].

■ Information is disclosed in accordance with s.55(4) if disclosed:

• under an order of the Court of Session or a Sheriff;

• to an adopted person who is aged 16 or over and to whom the information relates; or

• to a local authority, Board, registered adoption society or relevant adoption society which is providing counselling for any such adopted person [s.55(4)].

■ When the Registrar General discloses information to an adopted person aged 16 or over to whom the information relates, the Registrar must inform the adopted person that counselling services are available for the person:

• if the person is in Scotland, from any local authority in Scotland;

• if the person is in England and Wales, from any local authority in England and Wales;

• if the person is in Northern Ireland, from any Board;

• if the person is in the United Kingdom and the person's adoption was arranged by a registered adoption service, from that service; a registered adoption society, from that society; or a relevant adoption society, from that society [s.55(5)].

- When in accordance with s.55(4) information is disclosed to an adopted person who is in Scotland, or such a person applies for information under Schedule 2 Adoption and Children Act 2002, or Article 54 of the Northern Ireland Order, any body mentioned below in s.55(7) from which the adopted person requests counselling must provide counselling for the person [s.55(6)].

- Those bodies are:

  - any local authority in Scotland;

  - any registered adoption service; or

  - any registered adoption society or relevant adoption society in so far as (by virtue of s.76(2)) that society is acting as an adoption society in Scotland [s.55(7)].

- In s.55:

  - "Board" means a Health and Social Services Board established under Article 16 of the Health and Personal Social Services (Northern Ireland) Order 1972 (S.I. 1972/1265);

  - "Local authority", in relation to England and Wales, means any unitary authority, or any county council so far as it is not a unitary authority;

  - "Relevant adoption society" means an adoption society registered under Article 4 of the Northern Ireland Order [s.55(8)].

Admissibility of extracts as evidence [s.56]
- An extract of an entry in the Adopted Children Register is sufficient evidence of the adoption to which it relates and when an entry in the Adopted Children Register contains a record of the date of birth, or country of the birth of the adopted person, an extract of the entry issued by virtue of that section is sufficient evidence of that date or, as the case may be, country.

Adoptions with a foreign element

RESTRICTIONS ON MOVEMENT OF CHILDREN
Restrictions on bringing children into the UK [s.58]

- S.58 applies where a person who is habitually resident in the British Islands (the "British resident"):

  - brings, or causes another to bring, a child who is habitually resident outwith the British Islands into the UK for the purpose of adoption by the British resident, or

  - at any time brings, or causes another to bring, into the UK a child adopted by the British resident under an external adoption effected within the period of 12 months ending with that time [s.58(1)].

- In s.58(1), references to adoption, or a child adopted, by the British resident include a reference to adoption, or a child adopted, by the British resident and another person [s.58(2)].

- S.58 does *not* apply if the child is intended to be adopted under a Convention adoption order [s.58(3)].

- An external adoption means an adoption, other than a Convention adoption, of a child effected under the law of any country or territory outwith the British Islands, whether or not the adoption is:

  - an adoption within the meaning of Chapter 3, or

  - a full adoption (as defined in s.40(8)) [s.58(4)].

- Regulations may require a person intending to bring, or to cause another to bring, a child into the UK in circumstances when s.58 applies, to:

  - apply to an adoption agency in the prescribed manner for an assessment of the person's suitability to adopt the child, and

- give the agency any information it may require for the purpose of the assessment [s.58(5)].

■ Regulations may require prescribed conditions to be met in respect of a child brought into the UK in circumstances when s.58 applies [s.58(6)].

■ In relation to a child brought into the UK for adoption in circumstances when s.58 applies, regulations may provide for any provision of the adoption process to apply with modifications or not to apply [s.58(7)].

■ Regulations may provide for s.58 not to apply if any prescribed conditions are met and:

- the adopters or, as the case may be, prospective adopters of the child in question are natural parents, natural relatives, or guardians of the child (or one of them is), or

- the British resident in question is a step-parent of the child [s.58(8)].

■ On the occasion of the first exercise of the power to make regulations under s.58(8):

- the regulations must not be made unless a draft of the regulations has been approved by a resolution of the Scottish Parliament, and

- accordingly s.117(4) does not apply to the statutory instrument containing the regulations [s.58(9)].

Preliminary order where child to be adopted abroad [s.59]

■ The appropriate court may, on an application by persons ("the prospective adopters") who the court is satisfied intend to adopt a child under the law of a country or territory outwith the British Islands, make an order vesting parental responsibilities and parental rights in relation to the child in the prospective adopters [s.59(1)].

■ If the court is satisfied that the prospective adopters would meet the requirements as to domicile, or habitual residence, in Scotland which they would require to meet if an adoption order were to be made on their application, the court may not make an order under s.59 [s.59(2)].

■ An order under s.59 may not be made unless any requirements prescribed by regulations by the Scottish Ministers are satisfied [s.59(3)].

■ An application for an order under s.59 may not be made unless at all times during the period of 10 weeks immediately preceding the application the child's home was with the prospective adopters [s.59(4)].

■ S.35 (effect of order on existing rights etc) has effect in relation to an order under s.59 as it has effect in relation to adoption orders [s.59(5)].

■ The Scottish Ministers may by regulations provide for any provision of this Act which relates to adoption orders to apply, with or without modifications, to orders under s.59 [s.59(6)].

Restriction on removal of children for adoption outwith Great Britain [s.60]

■ A person who takes or sends a protected child out of Great Britain to any place outwith the British Islands with a view to the adoption of the child by any person commits an offence [s.60(1)].

■ A person who makes or takes part in any arrangements for transferring the care of a protected child to another person, knowing that the other person intends to take or send the child out of Great Britain in circumstances which would constitute an offence under s.60(1), commits an offence [s.60(2)].

■ No offence is committed under s.60(1) if the child is taken or sent out of Great Britain under the authority of an order under:

  • s.59;

  • s.84 of the Adoption and Children Act 2002; or

- Article 57 of the Northern Ireland Order [s.60(3)].

■ A person is deemed take part in arrangements for transferring the care of a child to another person for the purpose mentioned in s.60(2) if the person:

  - facilitates the placing of the child in the care of the other person;

  - initiates or takes part in negotiations the purpose or effect of which is the making of such arrangements, or the conclusion of an agreement to transfer the care of the child, for the purpose mentioned in s.60(2)]; or

  - causes any person to initiate or take part in any such negotiations [s.60(4)].

■ The Scottish Ministers may by regulations provide for s.60(1) to (3) to apply with modifications, or not to apply, if as well as any conditions prescribed by the regulations being met, the:

  - prospective adopters are parents, relatives, or guardians of the child (or one of them is), or

  - prospective adopter is a step-parent of the child [s.60(5)].

■ On the occasion of the first exercise of the power to make regulations under s.60(5):

  - the regulations must not be made unless a draft of the regulations has been approved by a resolution of the Scottish Parliament; and

  - accordingly s.117(4) does not apply to the statutory instrument containing the regulations [s.60(6)].

■ In any proceedings under s.60:

  - a report by a British consular officer or a deposition made before, and authenticated under the signature of, such an officer is (if proved that the officer or deponent cannot be found in the UK) sufficient evidence of the matters stated in the report or deposition; and

- it is not necessary to prove the signature or official character of the person who bears to have signed the report or deposition [s.60(7)].

■ A person who commits an offence under s.60 is liable on summary conviction to imprisonment for a term not exceeding 3 months or a fine not exceeding level 5 on the standard scale or both [s.60(8)].

■ In s.60(1) and (2), "protected child" means a child who is habitually resident in the UK, or a Commonwealth citizen [s.60(9)].

Regulations under s.58: offences [s.61]

■ A person who brings, or causes another to bring, a child into the UK at any time in circumstances when s.58 applies commits an offence if s/he has not:

- complied with any requirement imposed by virtue of s.58(5); or

- met any condition which the person is required to meet by virtue of s.58(6) [s.61(1)], before that time or before any later time which may be prescribed by regulations.

■ A person who commits an offence under subsection (1) is liable:

- on summary conviction to imprisonment for a term not exceeding 6 months or a fine not exceeding the statutory maximum or both;

- on conviction on indictment to imprisonment for a term not exceeding 12 months, or a fine or both [s.61(2)].

Adoptions from abroad: special restrictions

Declaration of special restrictions on adoptions from abroad [s.62]

■ S.62 applies if the Scottish Ministers have reason to believe that, because of practices taking place in a country or territory outwith the British Islands (the "relevant country") in connection with the adoption of children, it would be contrary to public policy to further the bringing of children into the UK in the cases mentioned in s.62(2) [s.62(1)].

- Those cases are that a British resident:

  - wishes to bring, or cause another to bring, a child who is not a British resident into the UK for the purpose of adoption by the British resident and, in connection with the proposed adoption, there have been, or would have to be, proceedings in the relevant country or dealings with authorities or agencies there, or

  - wishes to bring, or cause another to bring, into the UK a child adopted by the British resident under an adoption effected, within the period of 12 months ending with the date of the bringing in, under the law of the relevant country [s.62(2)].

- The Scottish Ministers may by order declare, in relation to any relevant country, that special restrictions are to apply for the time being in relation to the bringing in of children in the cases mentioned in s.62(2) [s.62(3)].

- The Scottish Ministers must, as respects each relevant country in relation to which such a declaration has effect for the time being (a "restricted country"), publish reasons for making the declaration in relation to the country [s.62(4)].

- The Scottish Ministers must publish a list of restricted countries ("the restricted list") and keep the list up to date [s.62(5)].

- The reasons and the restricted list are to be published in whatever way the Scottish Ministers think appropriate for bringing them to the attention of adoption agencies and members of the public [s.62(6)].

- In s.62, "British resident" means a person habitually resident in the British Islands and any reference to adoption by a British resident includes adoption by a British resident and another person [s.62(7);(8)].

Review [s.63]

- The Scottish Ministers must keep under review, in relation to each restricted country, whether it should continue to be a restricted country [s.63(1)].

- If the Scottish Ministers determine, in relation to a restricted country, that there is no longer a reason to believe what is mentioned in s.62(1), they must by order revoke the order containing the declaration made in relation to it under s.62(3) [s.63(2)].

The special restrictions [s.64]

- The special restrictions mentioned in s.62(3) are that the Scottish Ministers are not to take any step which they might otherwise have taken in connection with furthering the bringing of a child into the UK in the cases mentioned in s.62(2) (whether or not that step is provided for by virtue of any enactment) [s.64(1)].

- Nothing in s.64(1) prevents the Scottish Ministers from taking those steps if, in any particular case, the prospective adopters or, as the case may be, the adopters satisfy the Scottish Ministers that they should take those steps despite the special restrictions [s.64(2)].

- The Scottish Ministers may make regulations providing for:

  - the procedure to be followed by them in determining whether or not they are satisfied as mentioned in s.64(2);

  - matters which they are to take into account when making such a determination (whether or not they also take other matters into account) [s.64(3)].

Imposition of extra conditions in certain cases [s.65]

- The Scottish Ministers may make regulations providing:

  - for them to specify in the restricted list, in relation to any restricted country, a step which is not otherwise provided for by virtue of any enactment but which, by virtue of the arrangements between the UK and that country, the Scottish Ministers normally take in connection with the bringing in of a child where that country is concerned, and

- that, if such a step has been so specified in relation to a restricted country, one or more conditions specified in the regulations are to be met in respect of a child brought into the UK in either of the cases mentioned in s.62(2) (reading the reference there to the "relevant country" as being to the restricted country in question) [s.65(1)]

- Those conditions are in addition to any provided for by virtue of s.58 (restrictions on bringing children into the UK), or any other enactment [s.65(2)].

- A person who brings, or causes another to bring, a child into the United Kingdom commits an offence if the person has not met any condition which the person is required to meet by virtue of the latter condition of s.65(1).

- S.65(3) does not apply if the step specified in the restricted list in relation to any country had already been taken before the publication of the restricted list [s.65(2)].

- A person who commits an offence under s.65(3) is liable:

  - on summary conviction to imprisonment for a term not exceeding 6 months or a fine not exceeding the statutory maximum or both;

  - on conviction on indictment to imprisonment for a term not exceeding 12 months or a fine or both [s.65(5)].

- In s.65, "restricted country" and "restricted list" have the same meanings as in s.62 [s.65(6)].

Charging

Power to charge [s.66]

- S.66 applies to adoptions to which s.58 applies, or to which regulations made under s.1 Adoption (Intercountry Aspects) Act 1999 apply [s.66(1)].

- The Scottish Ministers may charge a fee to adopters for services provided or to be provided by them in relation to adoptions to which this section applies [s.66(2)].

- The Scottish Ministers may determine the level of fee as they see fit and may, in particular:

  - charge a flat fee or charge different fees in different cases or descriptions of case;

  - in any case or description of case, waive a fee [s.66(3)].

- The Scottish Ministers must secure that, taking one financial year with another, the income from fees under s.66 does not exceed the total cost to them of providing the services in relation to which the fees are imposed [s.66(4)].

- In s.66 "financial year" means a period of 12 months ending with 31 March and any references to adoptions include prospective adoptions, and to adopters include prospective adopters [s.66(5);(6)].

Overseas adoptions etc

Meaning of "overseas adoption" [s.67]

- In this Act, "overseas adoption":

  - means an adoption of a description specified in regulations made by the Scottish Ministers (being a description of adoptions effected under the law of any country or territory outwith the British Islands); but

- does not include a Convention adoption [s.67(1)].

■ The Scottish Ministers may by regulations prescribe the requirements that ought to be met by an adoption of any description effected after the coming into force of the regulations for it to be an overseas adoption for the purposes of this Act [s.67(2)].

■ At any time when regulations under s.67(2) are in force, the Scottish Ministers must exercise their power under s.67(1) so as to secure that adoptions of any description effected after the coming into force of the regulations are not overseas adoptions for the purposes of this Act if they consider that such adoptions are not likely, within a reasonable time, to meet the requirements prescribed under s.67(2) [s.67(3)].

■ Regulations under s.67(1) may contain provision as to the manner in which evidence of any overseas adoption may be given [s.67(4)].

■ In this section, "adoption" means the adoption of a child or of a person who was a child at the time the adoption was applied for [s.67(5)].

Annulment and recognition [s.68]

■ The Court of Session may, on an application under this subsection, by order annul a Convention adoption or a Convention adoption order on the ground that the adoption or, as the case may be, order is contrary to public policy [s.68(1)].

■ The Court of Session may, on an application under s.68(2):

- order an overseas adoption or a determination is to cease to be valid in Great Britain on the ground that the adoption or, as the case may be, determination is contrary to public policy or that the authority which purported to authorise the adoption or make the determination was not competent to entertain the case;

- decide the extent, if any, to which a determination has been affected by a subsequent determination [s.68(2)].

■ The Court of Session may, in any proceedings in that court, decide an overseas adoption or a determination is, for the purposes of those proceedings, to be treated as invalid in Great Britain on either of the grounds mentioned in the first para. of s.68(2) above [s.68(3)].

■ An order or decision of the High Court on an application under s.89(2) of the Adoption and Children Act 2002 is to be recognised and to have effect as if it were an order or decision of the Court of Session on an application under s.68(2) [s.68(4)].

■ Except as provided by s.68 the validity of a Convention adoption, a Convention adoption order, an overseas adoption or a determination is not to be questioned in proceedings in any court in Scotland [s.68(5)].

■ In s.68 "determination" means such a determination as is mentioned in s.70 [s.68(6)].

Supplementary provision [s.69]

■ Any application for an order under s.68, or a decision under the latter para. of s.68(2) is to be made in the manner prescribed in regulations made by the Scottish Ministers and within such period as may be so prescribed [s.69(1)].

■ No application is to be made under s.68(1) in respect of an adoption unless immediately before the application is made the person adopted was habitually resident in Scotland, or the persons on whose application the adoption order was made were habitually resident there [s.69(2)].

■ In deciding in pursuance of s.68 whether such an authority as is mentioned in s.70 was competent to hear a particular case, a court is to be bound by any finding of fact made by the authority and stated by the authority to be so made for the purpose of determining whether the authority was competent to hear the case [s.69(3)].

Effect of determinations and orders made outwith Scotland [s.70]

■ S.70(2) applies when an authority makes a determination (the "relevant determination") in the exercise of its power and that authority is:

- an authority of a Convention country (other than the UK) having power under the law of that country to authorise, or review the authorisation of, a Convention adoption, or to give or review a decision revoking or annulling such an adoption or a Convention adoption order; or

- an authority of a relevant territory having power under the law of that territory to authorise, or review the authorisation of, a Convention adoption or an adoption effected in that territory, or to give or review a decision revoking or annulling such an adoption or a Convention adoption order [s.70(1)].

■ Subject to s.68 and any subsequent determination having effect under this subsection, the relevant determination has effect in Scotland for the purpose of effecting, confirming or terminating the adoption in question or confirming its termination as the case may be [s.70(2)].

■ In s.70(1), "relevant territory" means any of the Channel Islands, the Isle of Man, or any British overseas territory (within the meaning of the British Nationality Act 1981 [s.70(3)].

■ S.35 applies in relation to an order under Article 17 (freeing child for adoption with parental agreement) or 18 (freeing child for adoption without parental agreement) of the Northern Ireland Order as if it were an adoption order [s.70(4)].

■ S.35(2) and (3) and s.43 apply in relation to a child who is the subject of an order which is similar to an order under s.59, and is made (whether before or after this Act has effect) in a part of the British Islands, as those sections apply in relation to a child who is the subject of an adoption order [s.70(5)].

Miscellaneous

ADOPTION ALLOWANCES
Adoption allowance schemes [s.71]

■ Subject to s.71(3), an adoption agency which is:

- a local authority *must*, within such period after the coming into force of s.71 as the Scottish Ministers may by order direct, prepare an adoption allowances scheme;

- a registered adoption service, may prepare such a scheme [s.71(1)].

Adoption allowances schemes had to be prepared on or before 28 December 2010 [The Period to Prepare an Adoption Allowances Scheme (Scotland) Regulations 2009].

■ An adoption allowances scheme is a scheme for or in connection with the payment by the agency of allowances to any person who has adopted, or intends to adopt, a child in any case where arrangements for the adoption were made or, as the case may be, are to be made by the agency [s.71(2)].

NB Adoption allowances schemes apply only to adoption agency placements.

■ The Scottish Ministers may by regulations (the Adoption Support Services and Allowances (Scotland) Regulations 2009) make provision for or in connection with adoption allowances schemes [s.71(3)].

■ Regulations under s.71(3) may in particular make provision for or in connection with specifying the:

- procedure to be followed by an agency in determining whether a person should be paid an allowance;

- circumstances in which an allowance may be paid;

- factors to be taken into account in determining the amount of an allowance;

- procedure for review, variation and termination of allowances;

- information about allowances which is to be supplied by an agency to a person who intends to adopt a child; and

- procedure to be followed by an agency in preparing, modifying or revoking an adoption allowances scheme [s.71(4)].

Prohibited payments

Prohibition of certain payments [s.72]

- S.72 applies to any payment (other than an excepted payment) which is made to any person for or in consideration of the:

  - adoption by that person of a child;

  - giving by that person of any consent required in connection with the adoption of a child;

  - transfer by that person of the care of a child with a view to the adoption of the child; or

  - making by that person of any arrangements for the adoption of a child [s.72(1)].

- A person commits an offence if s/he:

  - makes any payment to which s.72 applies;

  - agrees or offers to make any such payment;

  - receives, or agrees to receive, any such payment;

  - attempts to obtain any such payment [s.72(2)].

- A person who commits an offence under s.72(2) is liable on summary conviction to imprisonment for a term not exceeding 3 months or a fine not exceeding level 5 on the standard scale or both [s.72(3)].

- If a person is convicted of an offence under s.72(2), the court may, without prejudice to any power which it has to make any other order in relation to the child as respects whom the offence was committed, order the child to be removed to a place of safety until:

  - the child can be returned to the child's parent or guardian; or

  - other arrangements can be made for the child [s.72(4)].

- In s.72 "payment" includes reward, and "place of safety" has the meaning given by s.93(1) of the Children (Scotland) Act 1995 [s.72(5)].

Excepted payments [s.73]
- A payment is an excepted payment if it is made by virtue of, or in accordance with, provision made by virtue of this Act, the Adoption and Children Act 2002 or the Northern Ireland Order [s.73(1)].

- A payment is an excepted payment if it is made:

  - to an adoption agency by a parent or guardian of the child, or a person who adopts, or proposes to adopt, a child in respect of expenses reasonably incurred by the agency in connection with the adoption, or proposed adoption, of the child;

  - in respect of any legal or medical expenses incurred or to be incurred by any person in connection with an application which the person has made, or proposes to make, for an adoption order or an order under s.59;

  - authorised by the court to which an application for an adoption order is made;

  - by an adoption agency to another adoption agency in consideration of placing the child for adoption;

- by an adoption agency to a voluntary organisation for the time being approved for the purposes of this paragraph by the Scottish Ministers as a fee for the services of the organisation in putting the agency in touch with another adoption agency with a view to the making of arrangements between the adoption agencies for the adoption of a child [s.73(2)].

■ In s.73 "payment" includes reward [s.73(3)].

Disclosure of medical information about parents

Disclosure of medical information about parents [s.74]

■ The Scottish Ministers may by regulations (the Adoption (Disclosure of Information and Medical Information about Natural Parents) (Scotland) Regulations 2009) make provision for or in connection with disclosure of information about the health of the natural parents of a child who is to be, may be or has been adopted ("the relevant child") [s.74(1)].

■ In making regulations under s.74(1), the Scottish Ministers must secure that a person to whom information is disclosed by virtue of the regulations has a duty of confidentiality in relation to the information [s.74(2)].

■ Notwithstanding s.74(2), regulations under s.74(1) may include provision enabling a person to whom information is disclosed by virtue of the regulations, in such circumstances and to such an extent as may be specified in the regulations, to disclose the information to:

- the relevant child;

- persons who are to or may adopt, or have adopted, the relevant child [s.74(3)].

■ Regulations under s.74(1) may, in particular, include provision for or in connection with specifying the:

- descriptions of person by whom, and to whom, information may be disclosed;

- circumstances in which information may be disclosed;

- type of information which may, or may not, be disclosed;

- circumstances in which consent to disclosure of information need not be obtained;

- processing of information by a person to whom information is disclosed [s.74(4)].

■ In s.74(4) "processing" has the same meaning as in s.1(1) Data Protection Act 1998 [s.74(5)].

Restrictions on arranging adoptions and placing for adoption

Restriction on arranging adoptions and placing children [s.75]

■ Subject to subsection (2), a person other than an adoption agency commits an offence if s/he:

- makes arrangements for the adoption of a child; or

- places a child for adoption [s.75(1)].

■ S.75(1) does not apply if the person proposing to adopt the child or, as the case may be, the person with whom the child is placed is:

- a parent of the child;

- any other relative of the child; or

- where a parent of the child is a member of a relevant couple, the other member of the couple [s.75(2)].

■ A person who receives a child placed in contravention of s.75(1) knowing that the placement is with a view to the person's adopting the child commits an offence [s.75(3)].

- A person commits an offence if s/he takes part in the management or control of a body of persons which:

  - exists wholly or partly for the purpose of making arrangements for the adoption of children, and

  - is not an adoption agency [s.75(4)].

- A person who commits an offence under s.75 is liable on summary conviction to imprisonment for a term not exceeding 3 months or a fine not exceeding level 5 on the standard scale or both [s.75(5)].

- In any proceedings for an offence under s.75(4), proof of things done, or words written, spoken or published, by any person taking part in the management or control of the body of persons, or in making arrangements for the adoption of children on behalf of the body, is sufficient evidence of the purpose for which that body exists [s.75(6)].

- It is immaterial whether the things done, or the words written, spoken or published are carried out in the presence of a party to the proceedings [s.75(7)].

Adoption societies which are not registered adoption services [s.76]
- S.76(2) applies when:

  - an adoption society is a registered adoption society, or registered as respects Northern Ireland under Part III of the Health and Personal Social Services (Quality, Improvement and Regulation) (Northern Ireland) Order 2003 (S.I. 2003/431), and the society is not a registered adoption service [s.76(1)].

- Except to the extent that the society considers it necessary to do so in the interests of a person mentioned in s.3(1) of the Adoption and Children Act 2002 or, as the case may be, Article 3 of the Northern Ireland Order, it must not act as an adoption society in Scotland [s.76(2)].

Effects of orders and placing for adoption under Adoption and Children Act (England and Wales) 2002

Effect of certain orders made in England and Wales [s.77]

■ An adoption order (within the meaning of s.46(1) of the Adoption and Children Act 2002) has effect in Scotland as it has in England and Wales but as if any reference to the parental responsibility for the child were to the parental responsibilities and parental rights in relation to the child [s.77(1)].

■ An order made under s.21 of that Act (placement orders), and the variation or revocation of such an order under s.23 or s.24 of that Act, have effect in Scotland as they have in England and Wales but as if any reference to the parental responsibility for the child were to the parental responsibilities and parental rights in relation to the child [s.77(2)].

Effect of placing for adoption etc under Adoption and Children Act 2002 [s.78]

■ S.25 (parental responsibility) and s.28(2) to (4) (further consequences of placement) of the 2002 Act have effect in Scotland as they have in England and Wales but with the modifications specified in s.78(2) below, if:

- a child is placed for adoption under s.19 of the 2002 Act (placing children with parental consent), or

- an adoption agency is authorised to place a child for adoption under that section [s.78(1)].

■ Those modifications are:

- in s.25, any reference to the parental responsibility for the child is to be read as a reference to the parental responsibilities and parental rights in relation to the child, and

• in s.28(2), the reference to the court is to be read as a reference to the appropriate court [s.78(2)].

Further consequences of placement and placement orders [s.79]
■ S.79(2) applies when:

  • a child is placed for adoption under s.19 of the 2002 Act (placing children with parental consent), or

  • an adoption agency is authorised to place a child for adoption under that section [s.79(1)].

■ No order under s.11(1) Children (Scotland) Act 1995 (court orders relating to parental responsibilities etc.) of a kind mentioned in s.11(2)(c) to (f) (residence orders, contact orders, specific issue orders and interdicts) may be made in respect of the child [s.79(2)].

■ On the making of an order under s.21 of the 2002 Act (a "placement order") in respect of a child, any order under s.11(1) of the 1995 Act of a kind mentioned in s.11(2)(c) to (f) (residence orders, contact orders, specific issue orders and interdicts) in respect of the child ceases to have effect [s.79(3)].

■ When a placement order is in force no such order as is mentioned in s.79(3), and no order under s.55 of the Children (Scotland) Act 1995 (child assessment orders), may be made in respect of the child [s.79(4)].

The making of permanence orders

Permanence orders [s.80]
■ The appropriate court may, on the application of a local authority, make a permanence order in respect of a child [s.80(1)].

The "appropriate court" is defined in s.118.

■ A permanence order is an order consisting of:

- the mandatory provision;

- such of the ancillary provisions as the court thinks fit; and

- if the conditions in s.83 are met, provision granting authority for the child to be adopted [s.80(2)].

■ In making a permanence order in respect of a child, the appropriate court must secure that each parental responsibility and parental right in respect of the child vests in a person [s.80(3)].

Permanence orders: mandatory provision [s.81]

■ The mandatory provision is provision vesting in the local authority for the appropriate period:

- the responsibility mentioned in s.1(1)(b)(ii) of the Children (Scotland) Act 1995 (provision of guidance appropriate to child's stage of development) in relation to the child, and

- the right mentioned in s.2(1)(a) of that Act (regulation of child's residence) in relation to the child [s.81(1)].

■ In s.81(1) "the appropriate period" means:

- in the case of the responsibility to provide guidance to the child, the period beginning with the making of the permanence order and ending with the day on which the child reaches the age of 18;

- in the case of the right to regulate the child's residence, the period beginning with the making of the permanence order and ending with the day on which the child reaches the age of 16 [s.81(2)].

Permanence orders: ancillary provisions [s.82]

■ The ancillary provisions are provisions:

- vesting in the local authority for the appropriate period such of the parental responsibilities mentioned in s.1(1)(a), (b)(i) and (d) of the Children (Scotland) Act 1995 and such of the parental rights mentioned in s.2(1)(b) and (d) of that Act relating to the child as the court considers appropriate;

- vesting in a person other than the local authority for the appropriate period such of the parental responsibilities mentioned in s.1(1) of that Act and such of the parental rights mentioned in s.2(1)(b) to (d) of that Act in relation to the child as the court considers appropriate;

- extinguishing any parental responsibilities which, immediately before the making of the order, vested in a parent or guardian of the child, and which by virtue of the making of the permanence order with mandatory and ancillary provisions now vest in the local authority or vest in another person;

- extinguishing any parental rights in relation to the child which, immediately before the making of the order, vested in a parent or guardian of the child, and which by virtue of the making of the permanence order with mandatory and ancillary provisions now vest in the local authority, or vest in another person;

- specifying such arrangements for contact between the child and any other person as the court considers appropriate and to be in the best interests of the child; and

- determining any question which has arisen in connection with any parental responsibilities or parental rights in relation to the child, or any other aspect of the welfare of the child [s.82(1)].

In s.82 "the appropriate period" means:

- in the case of the responsibility mentioned in s.1(1)(b)(ii) of the 1995 Act [the provision of guidance to the child], the period beginning with the making of the permanence order and ending with the day on which the child reaches the age of 18;

- in any other case, the period beginning with the making of the

permanence order and ending with the day on which the child reaches
the age of 16 [s.82(2)].

Order granting authority for adoption: conditions [s.83]
■ The conditions referred to in s.80(2)(c) above are that:

• the local authority has, in the application for the permanence order,
requested that the order include provision granting authority for the child
to be adopted;

• the court is satisfied that the child has been, or is likely to be, placed for
adoption;

• in the case of each parent or guardian of the child, the court is satisfied
that the parent or guardian understands what the effect of making an
adoption order would be and consents to the making of such an order in
relation to the child, *or* the parent's or guardian's consent to the making
of such an order should be dispensed with on one of the grounds
mentioned in s.83(2) below;

• the court considers that it would be better for the child if it were to grant
authority for the child to be adopted than if it were not to grant such
authority [s.83(1)].

■ The grounds for dispensing with the parent or guardian's consent are:

• the parent or guardian is dead;

• the parent or guardian cannot be found or is incapable of giving consent;

• s.83(3) or (4) applies;

• when neither s.83(3) nor s.83(4) applies, the welfare of the child
otherwise requires the consent to be dispensed with [s.83(2)].

■ S.83(3) applies if the parent or guardian:

• has parental responsibilities or parental rights in relation to the child
other than those mentioned in ss.1(1)(c) and 2(1)(c) Children (Scotland)

Act 1995, i.e. other than the responsibility and right to direct contact; and

- is, in the opinion of the court, unable satisfactorily to discharge those responsibilities, or exercise those rights; and

- is likely to continue to be unable to do so [s.83(3)].

■ S.83(4) applies if:

- the parent or guardian has, by virtue of the making of a permanence order without authority to adopt, no parental responsibilities or parental rights in relation to the child; and

- it is unlikely that such responsibilities will be imposed on, or such rights given to the parent or guardian [s.83(4)].

■ In s.83(1)(c) and (2), "parent", in relation to the child in respect of whom the permanence order is to be made, means:

- a parent who has any parental responsibilities or parental rights in relation to the child; or

- a parent who, by virtue of a permanence order which does not include provision granting authority for the child to be adopted, has no such responsibilities or rights [s.83(5)].

Conditions and considerations applicable to making order [s.84]

■ Except where s.84(2) applies, a permanence order may not be made in respect of a child who is aged 12 or over unless the child consents [s.84(1)].

■ S.84(2) applies when the court is satisfied that the child is incapable of consenting to the order [s.84(2)].

■ The court may not make a permanence order in respect of a child unless it considers that it would be better for the child that the order be made than that it should not be made [s.84(3)].

- In considering whether to make a permanence order and, if so, what provision the order should make, the court is to regard the need to safeguard and promote the welfare of the child throughout childhood as the paramount consideration [s.84(4)].

- Before making a permanence order, the court must:

  - after taking account of the child's age and maturity, so far as is reasonably practicable, give the child the opportunity to indicate whether s/he wishes to express any views, and if the child does so wish, give her/him the opportunity to express them;

  - have regard to any such views the child may express, the child's religious persuasion, racial origin and cultural and linguistic background, and the likely effect on her/him of the making of the order; and

  - be satisfied that there is no person who has the right mentioned in s.2(1)(a) Children (Scotland) Act 1995 to have the child living with the person or otherwise to regulate her/his residence; or if there is such a person, be satisfied that the child's residence with the person is, or is likely to be, seriously detrimental to the welfare of the child [s.84(5)].

  A child aged 12 or over is presumed to be of sufficient age and maturity to form a view for the purposes of s.84(5) [s.84(6)].

Child in respect of whom order may be made [s.85]

- A permanence order may be made in respect of a child who is an adopted child [s.85(1)].

- A permanence order may not be made in respect of a child who is or has been married or a civil partner [s.85(2)].

Representations [s.86]

- In any proceedings relating to an application for a permanence order, the appropriate court must permit any person mentioned in s.86(2) who wishes to make representations to the court to do so [s.86(1)].

■ Those persons are:

- the local authority making the application;

- the child or the child's representative;

- any person who has parental responsibilities or parental rights in relation to the child;

- any other person who claims an interest [s.86(2)].

Effect of order

Effect of order on existing parental right [s.87]

■ The making of a permanence order extinguishes the parental right mentioned in s.2(1)(a) Children (Scotland) Act 1995 (the right to control the child's residence) of a parent of the child in respect of whom the order is made, or of a guardian of such a child, which immediately before the making of the order vested in the parent or guardian [s.87].

Effect of order on existing orders [s.88]

■ S.88 applies when:

- parental responsibilities or parental rights in relation to a child vest in a person by virtue of a permanence order, or an order under s.11 Children (Scotland) Act 1995, ("the existing order"), and

- the appropriate court intends to make a permanence order ("the new order") as respects the child [s.88(1)].

■ On the making of the new order, the existing order is revoked [s.88(2)].

■ In making the new order, the court must secure that the parental responsibilities or parental rights vesting by virtue of the existing order vest in a person under the new order [s.88(3)].

Revocation of supervision requirement

Revocation of supervision requirement [s.89]

- S.89(2) applies when the:

  - child in respect of whom a permanence order is to be made is subject to a supervision requirement, and

  - the appropriate court is satisfied that, were it to make a permanence order in respect of the child, compulsory measures of supervision in respect of the child would no longer be necessary [s.89(1)].

- The court must make an order providing that, on the making of the permanence order, the supervision requirement ceases to have effect [s.89(2)].

Precedence

Precedence of court orders and supervision requirements over order [s.90]

- S.90(2) applies where a local authority has, by virtue of a permanence order, parental responsibilities or parental rights in relation to a child [s.90(1)].

- The local authority must not act in any way which would be incompatible with:

  - any other court order of which the authority is aware relating to the child or the child's property;

  - any supervision requirement to which the child is subject [s.90(2)].

Exercise of parental right under order

Exercise of parental right under order [s.91]

■ S.91(2) applies when:

- two or more persons have a parental right in relation to a child, and

- by virtue of s.82(1) the right vests in one of them or, as the case may be, two or more of them [s.91(1)].

■ Each of the persons mentioned above may exercise the right without the consent of the other or, as the case may be, any of the others [s.91(2)].

■ S.91(2) does not apply where an order vesting the right, or regulating its exercise, provides otherwise [s.91(3)].

Variation

Variation of ancillary provision in order [s.92]

■ S.92 applies when a permanence order which includes ancillary provisions is in force [s.92(1)].

■ The appropriate court may, on an application by a person mentioned in s.92(3), vary such of the ancillary provisions as the court considers appropriate [s.92(2)].

■ Those persons are:

- the local authority on whose application the permanence order was made;

- if the child in respect of whom the order was made is aged 12 or over, or under the age of 12 but, in the court's opinion (taking account of the child's age and maturity), capable of understanding the effect of the order, that child;

- any person in whom parental responsibilities and parental rights are vested by virtue of the order;

- any person in whom were vested, immediately before the making of the order, any parental responsibilities or parental rights which, by virtue of the making of the order, vest in another person;

- any person in whom were vested, immediately before a variation by virtue of this section of the order, parental responsibilities or parental rights which, by virtue of the variation, vest in another person;

- any other person who claims an interest [s.92(3)].

■ S.92(5) applies where the court exercises its power under s.92(2) to vary the ancillary provisions so as to vest, by virtue of s.82(1), in a person a parental responsibility or a parental right which, immediately before the variation, vested in another person [s.92(4)].

■ The court may include in the order as varied provision extinguishing the responsibility or right of that other person [s.92(5)].

■ S.84(4), (5)(a) and (b) and (6) apply to the variation of a permanence order under s.92 as they apply to the making of such an order [s.92(6)].

■ In s.92(1) and (2), "ancillary provisions" has the same meaning as in s.82 [s.92(7)].

■ In s.92, "vary" includes add to, omit, or amend; and "variation" is to be construed accordingly [s.92(8)].

Amendment of order to grant authority for child to be adopted [s.93]

■ S.93 applies when:

- a permanence order in respect of a child is in force; and

- the order does not include provision granting authority for the child to be adopted [s.93(1)].

- On the application of the local authority on whose application the order was made, the appropriate court may amend the order so as to include provision granting authority for the child to be adopted if (and only if) the court:

  - is satisfied that the child has been placed for adoption, or is likely to be placed for adoption;

  - is satisfied that the condition in s.93(3) or (4) below is met; and

  - considers that it would be better for the child that authority for the child to be adopted is granted than that it should not be granted [s.93(2)].

- The condition is that each parent or guardian of the child understands what the effect of making an adoption order would be and consents to the making of such an order in relation to the child [s.93(3)].

- The condition is that the consent of each parent or guardian should be dispensed with on any of the grounds mentioned in s.83 [s.93(4)].

- S.84(4), (5)(a) and (b) and (6) apply to the amendment of a permanence order under s.93 as they apply to the making of such an order [s.93(5)].

- In s.93(3) and (4):

  - "Guardian", in relation to a child in respect of whom a permanence order to which s.93 applies is in force, means a guardian who has any parental responsibilities or parental rights in relation to the child, or who, by virtue of the making of a previous such order, no longer has any such responsibilities or rights;

  - "Parent", in relation to a child in respect of whom a permanence order to which s.93 applies is in force, means a parent who has any parental responsibilities or parental rights in relation to the child, or who, by virtue of the making of a previous such order, no longer has any such responsibilities or rights [s.93(6)].

Proceedings [s.94]

■ In any proceedings for variation of a permanence order by the local authority on whose application the order was granted, the appropriate court must permit any person who is affected by the order, and who wishes to make representations to the court, to do so [s.94(1)].

■ In any proceedings for variation of a permanence order by a person other than the local authority on whose application the order was granted, the appropriate court must permit any person mentioned in s.94(3) who wishes to make representations to the court to do so [s.94(2)].

■ Those persons are:

- the local authority on whose application the permanence order was made;

- if the child in respect of whom the original order was made is aged 12 or over, or under the age of 12 but, in the court's opinion (taking account of the child's age and maturity), is capable of understanding the effect of the order, that child;

- any person who has parental responsibilities or parental rights in relation to the child;

- any person on whom a duty was imposed, or power conferred, by the order;

- any person in whom were vested, immediately before the making of the order, any parental responsibilities or parental rights which, by virtue of the making of the order, vest in another person;

- any person in whom were vested, immediately before a variation by virtue of s.92 of the order, parental responsibilities or parental rights which, by virtue of the variation, vest in another person;

- any other person who claims an interest [s.94(3)].

■ A person other than the local authority on whose application a permanence order was granted may not apply to the court for a variation of the order without first obtaining the leave of the court [s.94(4)].

- The court must grant that leave if it is satisfied that:

  - there has been a material change in the circumstances directly relating to any of the order's provisions, or

  - for any other reason it is proper to allow the application to be made [s.94(5)].

- In determining whether there has been a material change in circumstances, the court must have regard, in particular, to any aspect of:

  - the welfare of the child in respect of whom the permanence order was made; and

  - the circumstances of a parent, or the parents, of the child, the child's guardian; or

  - any person mentioned in the 5th and 6th bullet points of s.94(3) above [s.94(6)].

- In s.94(1), the reference to variation of a permanence order includes a reference to amendment of the order to include provision granting authority for the child to whom the order relates to be adopted [s.94(7)].

Orders and supervision requirements

Duty of children's hearing to prepare report for court [s.95]
- S.95(2) applies when:

  - an application is made for a permanence order, or variation of such an order, in respect of a child;

  - the application has not been determined (or, as the case may be, withdrawn or abandoned); and

- a Children's Hearing proposes to make a supervision requirement in respect of the child, or modify, under s.73(9)(c) or (d) Children (Scotland) Act 1995, a supervision requirement that has been made in respect of the child [s.95(1)].

■ The Children's Hearing must prepare for the court to which the application has been made a report containing such information as the Scottish Ministers may by regulations prescribe [s.95(2)] – see S.I. 2009/169, The Adoption and Children (Scotland) Act 2007 (Supervision Requirement Reports in Applications for Permanence Orders) Regulations 2009.

■ In s.95(1), the reference to variation of a permanence order includes a reference to amendment of the order to include provision granting authority for the child to whom the order relates to be adopted [s.95(3)].

Application: effect on supervision requirement [s.96]
■ S.96(2) applies when an application is made for a permanence order, or variation of such an order, in respect of a child [s.96(1)].

■ A supervision requirement in respect of the child may not be made, or modified under s.73(9) Children (Scotland) Act 1995 until the application is determined (or, as the case may be, withdrawn or abandoned) [s.96(2)].

■ S.96(2) does not apply if the court to which the application is made refers the child's case to the Principal Reporter (whether following receipt of a report under s.95 or otherwise) [s.96(3)].

■ In s.96(1), the reference to variation of a permanence order includes a reference to amendment of the order to include provision granting authority for the child to whom the order relates to be adopted [s.96(4)].

■ In s.96(3), "Principal Reporter" has the same meaning as in Part II of the Children (Scotland) Act 1995 [s.96(5)].

Interim orders and revocation of supervision requirement [s.97]

- When an application is made for a permanence order, or variation of such an order, in respect of a child the appropriate court may make such interim order as it thinks fit [s.97(1) and (2)].

- The court must make an order providing that, on the making of the interim order, the supervision requirement ceases to have effect when the:

  - child in respect of whom an interim order is to be made is subject to a supervision requirement, and

  - court is satisfied that, were it to make an interim order in relation to the child, compulsory measures of supervision in respect of the child would no longer be necessary [s.97(3) and (4)].

- The provisions of the order prevail if the:

  - child in respect of whom an interim order is made is subject to a supervision requirement, and

  - provisions of the order conflict, or are otherwise inconsistent, with the supervision requirement [s.97(5)].

- In s.97(1), the reference to variation of a permanence order includes a reference to amendment of the order to include provision granting authority for the child to whom the order relates to be adopted [s.97(6)].

Revocation and variation

Revocation [s.98]

- The appropriate court may, on an application by the local authority on whose application the order was made or any other person affected by the order who has obtained the leave of the court to apply for revocation of the order, revoke a permanence order if satisfied it is appropriate to do so in all the circumstances of the case, including, in particular:

- a material change in the circumstances directly relating to any of the order's provisions, and

- any wish by the parent or guardian of the child in respect of whom the order was made to have reinstated any parental responsibilities or parental rights vested in another person by virtue of the order [s.98(1) and (2)]

■ In considering whether to revoke a permanence order, the court is to regard the need to safeguard and promote the welfare of the child throughout childhood as the paramount consideration and before revoking the order, the court must:

- after taking account of the child's age and maturity, so far as is reasonably practicable, give the child the opportunity to indicate whether s/he wishes to express any views, and if the child does so wish, give her/him the opportunity to express them;

- have regard to any such views the child may express, the child's religious persuasion, racial origin and cultural and linguistic background, and the likely effect on her/him of the making of the order [s.98(3)].

A child aged 12 or over is presumed to be of sufficient age and maturity to form a view for the purposes of s.98.

Duty of local authority to apply for variation or revocation [s.99]
■ When a local authority on whose application a permanence order was made determines that there has been a material change in the circumstances directly relating to any of the order's provisions, and in consequence of that change, the order ought to be varied or revoked:

- the authority must, as soon as is reasonably practicable, apply to the appropriate court for variation or, as the case may be, revocation of the order [s.99(1) and (2)].

In s.99 "variation", in relation to the permanence order, includes amendment of the order so as to include provision granting authority for the child to whom the order relates to be adopted; and "varied" is to be construed accordingly [s.99(3)].

Revocation under s.11 Children (Scotland) Act 1995 [s.100]

■ When the appropriate court revokes a permanence order in respect of a child it must consider whether to make an order under s.11 Children (Scotland) Act 1995 imposing on a person specified in the order parental responsibilities in relation to the child, and giving to such a person parental rights in relation to the child [s.100(1) and (2)].

Notification requirements

Local authority to give notice of certain matters [s.101]

■ S.101 applies where:

- a permanence order includes provision granting authority for the child to be adopted; and

- after the order is made or amended under s.93(2) so as to include that provision, an "event" mentioned in s.101(2) occurs; and

- the order has not been revoked under s.98(1) [s.101(1)].

■ Those "events" are:

- the child is placed for adoption;

- an adoption order is made in respect of the child;

- the child ceases to be placed for adoption otherwise than on the making of an adoption order [s.101(2)].

■ As soon as is reasonably practicable after the occurrence of the event, the local authority on whose application the permanence order was made must give notice of the event to any person:

- who consented under s.83(1)(c)(i) or s.93(3) to the making of the permanence order;

- whose consent to the making of the permanence order was dispensed with under s.83(1)(c)(ii) or s.93(4) [s.101(3) and (4)].

The local authority need not comply with the requirement imposed by s.101(3) in relation to a person if the person has given notice to that effect to the authority [s.101(5)].

Effect of subsequent adoption order on permanence order

Effect of subsequent adoption order on permanence order [s.102]

■ When a permanence order is in force and an adoption order is made in respect of the child, the permanence order ceases to have effect [s.102(1) and (2)].

Restriction on making certain orders under 1995 Act

Restriction on making orders under s.11 [s.103]

■ Where a permanence order is in force, a court may not make under s.11(1) of the 1995 Act any order mentioned in s11(2)(a) to (e) of the 1995 Act [s.103].

Rules of procedure

Permanence orders: rules of procedure [s.104]

■ Provision may be made by rules of court in respect of applications for:

- permanence orders;

- variation, or revocation, of permanence orders;

- applications for leave to apply for such variation or revocation.

■ In the case of an application for a permanence order containing a request that the order include provision granting authority for the child to be adopted, or an application made by virtue of s.93(2) (amendment of permanence order to grant authority for child to be adopted), rules must require:

- every person who can be found and whose consent to the making of the order is required to be given or dispensed with under this Act or, if no such person can be found, any relative prescribed by the rules who can be found, to be notified of all the matters mentioned in s.104(4), and

- the child's father (if he can be found, and does not have, and has never had, parental responsibilities or parental rights in relation to the child), to be notified only that the application has been made, and the date and location of the hearing [s.104(2) and (3)].

■ The matters listed in s.104(4) are:

- that the application has been made;

- the date on which, and place where, the application will be heard;

- the Permanence Orders: Rules of Procedure [s.104] act that the person is entitled to be heard on the application; and

- the fact that, unless the person wishes, or the court requires, the person need not attend the hearing [s.104(4)].

In s.104(1), any references to an application for variation of a permanence order include references to an application to amend the order to include provision granting authority for the child to whom the order relates to be adopted [s.104(5)]. See S.I. 2009/283 for the Rules of the Court of Session; and S.I. 2009/284 for the Sheriff Court Rules.

Miscellaneous

PROVISIONS APPLICABLE TO ADOPTION ORDERS AND PERMANENCE ORDERS
Notification of proposed application for order [s.105]

■ S.105(2) applies when:

- a local authority proposes to make an application for a permanence order in respect of a child; or

- becomes aware that an application for an adoption order in respect of a child in its area has been, or is to be made;

- the father of the child is not married to the mother of the child on the relevant date and never having had parental responsibilities or parental rights in relation to the child, does not have such responsibilities or rights on the relevant date, and the authority knows his identity and whereabouts, or can, by taking such reasonable and practicable steps as are appropriate in the circumstances of the case, ascertain that information [s.105(1)].

■ The local authority must, on or after the relevant date:

- give notice to the father that it proposes to apply for a permanence order or an application for an adoption order has been made, or an application for an adoption order is to be made (as the case may be), and

- provide the father with prescribed information relating to the processes for applying for the order in question [s.105(2)] – see S.I. 2010/172, The Adoption Agencies (Scotland) Amendment Regulations 2010.

■ When a local authority is required to give notice under s.105(2) that it proposes to apply for a permanence order, it must give the notice at least 4 weeks before the application for the permanence order is made [s.105(3)].

■ When a local authority is required to give notice that an application for an adoption order has been or is to be made, it must give the notice as soon as is reasonably practicable after it becomes aware that the application for an adoption order has been/is to be made [s.105(4)].

In s.105 "relevant date" means the date on which the local authority determines it will make the application for a permanence order or the date on which the authority becomes aware that an application for an adoption order in respect of a child in its area has been/is to be made and "prescribed" means prescribed by Regulations made by the Scottish Ministers [s.105(5)] – see S.I. 2010/172, The Adoption Agencies (Scotland) Amendment Regulations 2010.

Child subject to supervision: duty to refer to principal reporter [s.106]

- The registered adoption service must refer the child's case to the Principal Reporter if with respect to a child subject to a supervision requirement it:

  - is satisfied the best interests of the child would be served by placing the child for adoption, and

  - it intends to place the child for adoption [s.106(1) and (2)].

The Scottish Ministers may make regulations (the Adoption Agencies (Scotland) Regulations 2009) specifying by reference to the occurrence of an event or events described in the regulations the period of time during which a referral under s.106 is to be made. In s.106(2) "Principal Reporter" has the same meaning as in Part II of the Children (Scotland) Act.

Making of adoption order no longer to be bar to making of contact order [s.107]

- S.11 of the 1995 Act is amended whereby persons whose parental rights and responsibilities have been extinguished by the making of an adoption order, may apply for a contact order, but only with the leave of the court.

Rules: appointment of curators ad litem and reporting officers [s.108]

■ In the case of an application for a relevant order in relation to a child, rules of court must provide for the appointment, in such cases as are prescribed by the rules of a person to act as:

- curator ad litem of the child with the duty of safeguarding the interests of the child in such manner as may be so prescribed, and

- reporting officer for the purpose of witnessing agreements to adoption and performing such other duties as may be so prescribed [s.108(1)].

■ Rules may in particular make provision:

- enabling the reporting officer to be appointed before the application is made;

- enabling the court to appoint the same person to be curator ad litem and reporting officer [s.108(2)].

■ Rules may not make provision for:

- the appointment of a person who is employed by an adoption agency which has placed a child for adoption to act as curator ad litem or reporting officer for the purposes of an application for an adoption order in respect of the child;

- the appointment of a person who is employed by a local authority which is making (or has made) an application for a permanence order to act as curator ad litem or reporting officer for the purposes of the application [s.108(3)].

A relevant order means an adoption order, a permanence order, or an order under s.59 (preliminary order when child to be adopted abroad) [s.108(4)].

Proceedings to be in private [s.109]

■ Any of the following proceedings before the court must be heard and determined in private unless the court otherwise directs:

- s.24 (return of child removed in breach of certain provisions);

- s.29 (adoption by couples);

- s.30 (adoption by one person);

- s.59 (preliminary order when child to be adopted abroad);

- s.80 (permanence order);

- s.92 (variation of ancillary provisions in permanence order);

- s.93 (amendment of permanence order to grant authority for child to be adopted);

- s.99 (duty of local authority to apply for variation or revocation of permanence order).

Care allowances: regulations

Allowances for care of certain children: regulations [s.110]

- The Scottish Ministers may by regulations – see S.I. 2009/210 The Looked After Children (Scotland) Regulations 2009 – make provision about payments by a local authority in respect of a child who falls within s.110(2), i.e. one who:

  - is placed by the authority under s.26(1)(a) of the Children (Scotland) Act 1995; or

  - is required by virtue of s.70(3)(a) of that Act to reside with a person other than a parent of the child; or

  - were s/he not residing with a relative (it is immaterial whether or not the relative has parental rights and responsibilities [s.110(6)]), the authority would be required by s.25(1) of that Act to provide accommodation for the child [s.110(1) and (2)].

- Regulations under s.110(1) (see S.I. 2009/210 as above) may in particular include provision for or in connection with:

- specifying descriptions of persons to whom payments may be made;

- specifying circumstances in which payments may be made;

- specifying rates of payment to be payable in such circumstances as may be specified in the regulations;

- where a rate is so specified, requiring local authorities to pay at least that rate in the circumstances so specified, recommending that local authorities pay at least that rate ("the recommended rate") in the circumstances so specified;

- where a recommended rate is payable, requiring local authorities which pay less than that rate to publish, in such manner as may be so specified, their reasons for doing so [s.110(3)].

■ A child does not cease to be a child placed by the authority of s.26(1)(a) Children (Scotland) Act 1995 by reason only of the making of a permanence order vesting parental responsibilities in a person who is a member of the family with whom the child was placed [s.110(4)].

■ If the relative is a guardian of the child, the child does not fall within paragraph (c) of s.110(2) above [s.110(5)].

Evidence and notices

■ If a document signifying any consent required by this Act is witnessed in accordance with rules of court, it is sufficient evidence of the signature of the person by whom it was executed [s.111(1)].

■ A document signifying any such consent which purports to be witnessed in accordance with rules is to be presumed to be so witnessed and to have been executed and witnessed on the date and at the place specified in the document unless the contrary is shown [s.111(2)].

Service of notices etc [s.112]

■ Any notice or information required to be given under this Act may be given by post.

Admissibility of certain documents as evidence [s.113]

■ Any document which is receivable as evidence of any matter in England and Wales under s.77(4) and (5) of the 2002 Act, or in Northern Ireland under Article 63(1) of the Northern Ireland Order, is sufficient evidence in Scotland of the matter to which it relates.

Meaning of appropriate court [s.118]

■ In this Act, "appropriate court" means with respect to any application made by virtue of this Act:

- if the application relates to a child who is in Scotland when the application is made, the Court of Session, or the Sheriff Court of the Sheriffdom within which the child is;

- if the application is for an adoption order, or a permanence order seeking provision granting authority for the child to whom the order relates to be adopted, and s/he is not in Scotland when the application is made, the Court of Session [s.118(1)–(3)].

Sch.2 para. 9 of this Act introduced significant amendments to the Children (Scotland) Act 1995.

Part B

Regulations

The Adoption Agencies (Scotland) Regulations 2009

■ The Adoption Agencies (Scotland) Regulations govern the adoption functions of local authorities and registered adoption services in Scotland and came into force on 28 September 2009.

Adoption panel

■ Regulation 3 requires agencies to set up an adoption panel [reg.3.2] with at least 6 suitably qualified and experienced members [reg.3.5(a)], including a medical adviser and a legal adviser [reg.3.4 (a) and (b)]. Two or more agencies may establish a joint panel [reg.3.3]. An agency may terminate any member's membership after giving written notice, with reasons [reg.3.6]. Panel membership must be reviewed from time to time [reg.3.5(b)].

■ The quorum for meetings of the panel is 3 [reg.4.1] not including the legal or medical advisers [reg.4.4]. Where plans for adoption or plans for permanence order with authority to adopt for a child are being considered, the legal adviser must be present or have provided legal advice [reg.4.2]. Written minutes must be taken and include reasons for the panel's recommendations [reg.4.3].

■ Regulation 5 defines the qualification requirements for the appointment of medical and legal advisers, which are, respectively, a registered medical practitioner, and a solicitor or advocate.

■ Adoption panels must consider every child's case, proposed placement and prospective adopter referred by the agency [reg.6(a)–(c)], and recommend:

- a) if adoption is in a child's best interests;

- b) if the agency should apply for a permanence order with authority to place for adoption;

- c) if a prospective adopter is or continues to be suitable to adopt;

- d) if a particular match is suitable;

- e) in respect of any other relevant matter referred to the panel [reg.6.2].

■ Panels must have regard to the agency duties specified in s.14 of the Act, all the reports and information provided, and any necessary legal advice [reg.6.8].

■ When recommending adoption for a child, the written minute must include a note of the alternatives to adoption considered [reg.6.3], and if recommending contact with a parent [parent is defined in reg.6.9], reasons why continued contact is in the best interests of the child [reg.6.4].

There are different definitions of "parent" in these regulations. For the purposes of reg.6, a parent is one with parental responsibilities or rights in relation to the child. The definition in reg.14 also includes a parent without responsibilities or rights as a result of the making of a permanence order. The various provisions in reg.17 apply to the different groups there specified, in other words parents with PRRs get the notices, while parents without PRRs are subject only to enquiries by the local authority. Where the term is not defined it has the meaning "natural parents and those with parental rights and responsibilities".

■ The panel must give the opportunity for prospective adopters to meet the panel before recommending their suitability [reg.6.5], and cannot recommend a match unless both the plan for adoption and the suitability of the prospective adopters are being recommended at the same panel as the match or have previously been approved by the agency [reg.6.7].

Assessment and approval of prospective adopters

■ Agencies must publish their general criteria for determining suitability to adopt, and must review these from time to time [reg.7.1–2]. The criteria must be applied in determining a person's suitability along with any other steps the agency deems necessary [reg.7.2–3].

■ Where an applicant is not accepted for assessment as an adoptive parent, s/he must be given written notice [reg.7.4]. Where an applicant is accepted for assessment, the agency must:

- if possible, collect all the information specified in Sch. 1 Part 1 of these Regulations;

- carry out an assessment and prepare a report;

- refer the case to the panel with a copy of the report;

- notify the prospective adopter of the panel and provide a copy of the report (excluding any information provided by any person in confidence) [reg.7.5].

- Agencies must make a decision as to a prospective adopter's suitability within 14 days of receiving a panel recommendation, taking account of the recommendation, and being satisfied that s/he is a suitable person with whom to place children. No panel member may take part in the decision [reg.8(1)–(3)].

- If disagreeing with the panel's recommendation, the agency must record its reasons in writing [reg.8(4)].

- The agency must notify the prospective adopter in writing:

- within 14 days of making the decision that s/he is suitable to adopt; or

- within 7 days of making the decision that s/he is not suitable to adopt, giving reasons and enclosing a copy of the panel's recommendation if that was favourable [reg.8(5)–(6)(b)].

- In the latter case, the agency must also inform the prospective adopter of their right to require a review of the decision within 28 days of the notification and invite them to submit any representations within that time [reg.8(6)(c)–(d)].

View of agency decisions

- Prospective adopters may, within 28 days of a notice that they are not considered suitable to adopt, request a review of that decision [reg.9.1]. On receipt of such a request, the agency must refer the case to a differently constituted adoption panel, along with a copy of its decision and reasons, the original report, any representations received from the "appellant" and any further relevant information [reg.9.2–3].

■   The panel must consider the case and make a fresh recommendation as to suitability to adopt, and the agency then has 14 days to make a decision based on the new recommendation and a further 7 days to notify the applicant accordingly. If the decision is that s/he is not suitable, the agency must give reasons and enclose a copy of the panel's fresh recommendation if that was favourable [reg.9.4–6].

Review of adopters

■   Agencies must carry out a review of adopters they have approved if no child has been placed after 2 years, or where a child has been placed but no adoption application has been made and the agency considers a review necessary or appropriate for the child's welfare [reg.10(1)–(3)].

■   In reviewing approved adopters, agencies must reassess their suitability by making any enquiries and obtaining any information deemed necessary, and by seeking and taking account of the adopters' views [reg.10(4)].

■   If on review adopters may no longer be considered suitable, the agency must prepare a report on the reassessment and send it to the adopters, advising them that the case will be referred to the panel, and inviting them to make any representations within 14 days [reg.10(5)].

■   After 14 days (earlier if representations received before then) the agency must send the report and any representations to the panel, notify the adopters of the referral and provide a copy of the report excluding any information given by any person in confidence [reg.10(6)–(7)].

■   The panel must make a recommendation as to the adopters' continued suitability taking account of the review report, any representations and any other information the agency provides [reg.10(8)].

- Agencies must make a decision within 14 days of a panel recommendation on review under reg.10(8) and the same requirements apply as for suitability decisions under reg.8(2)–(6) and review of decisions under reg.9, i.e. time limits for notice of decision to be sent and adopters have the right to require a review by a differently constituted panel [reg.11].

Duties when considering a child's adoption

- When considering adoption for a child, agencies must (so far as reasonably practicable and in the child's best interests):

  - consult and take account of the child's views (depending on age and maturity) and those of parents and guardians whose whereabouts are known;

  - take account of the child's race, religion, culture and linguistic background;

  - obtain and record in writing the information required by Schedule 1 Parts II and III of these Regulations; and

  - arrange a medical examination and obtain a written health assessment [reg.12(1)–(2)].

- The agency must then refer any case where it thinks adoption is in a child's best interests to the panel, and provide the panel with the medical report, the Schedule 1 information, any representations from the child, parents or guardians, and any other relevant information [reg.12(3)–(4)].

Agency decisions and notifications

- Agencies must make a decision within 14 days of receipt of a panel recommendation, must take account of that recommendation, and must record reasons for any decision which departs from the recommendation. No panel member may take part in the decision [reg.13.1–4].

- Where the child is subject to a Supervision Requirement, local authority adoption agencies must take account of the panel's recommendation before deciding whether to apply for a permanence order, and all adoption agencies (including local authorities) or registered adoption services must do so before deciding whether to place a child for adoption [reg.13.5–7].

- Agencies must notify within 7 days of making a decision that adoption is in a child's best interests:

  - the child, if considered capable of understanding its effects;

  - the child's parent/s (with PRRs);

  - if considered in the child's best interests, any parent/s without parental rights or responsibilities whose whereabouts are known;

  - the child's guardian (if whereabouts known); and

  - any other relatives who have expressed views on the child's placement [reg.14.1].

- Agencies must notify within 7 days the child's parent/s (with PRRs), any parent/s without parental rights or responsibilities whose whereabouts are known (if considered in the child's best interests) and the child's guardian (if whereabouts known) of a decision about applying for a permanence order with authority to adopt [reg.14.2].

- Agencies must take any necessary steps consistent with the child's best interests if it decides a child should not be adopted because a better practicable alternative exists [reg.15(1)].

- Registered adoption services must refer a child to the local authority where the child lives having decided that an application for a permanence order with authority for the child to be adopted should be made [reg.15(2)].

Information to parents

- Regulations 16 and 17 cover the provision to parents of information about any decision that a child should be adopted or subject to a permanence order with authority to adopt application. The information must be provided in the form of the prescribed memorandum and accompanied by a certificate (for both memorandum and certificate see Schedules to these Regulations) acknowledging receipt and another indicating whether or not the parent agrees to the proposed action.

- Regulation 16 relates to decisions that adoption is in the child's best interests and proposals to place a child for adoption; the memorandum is Sch.2 and the certificates are Sch.3 and 4. These must be sent to the parent/s within 7 days of the decision.

- Regulation 17 deals with decisions to apply for a permanence order with authority to adopt and the memorandum and certificates are at Schs. 5, 6 and 7.

- In both cases agencies must take reasonable steps to ensure each parent signs and returns the certificates, and in the case of the certificate of agreement, does so within 28 days.

- Under both regs.16 and 17, where the adoption agency is aware of the identity of a parent without PRRs, it must make any reasonably practicable enquiries to obtain the information required by Sch.1 Part III (information about the child's family) and ascertain whether the parent intends to apply for parental rights or responsibilities or enter into a parental responsibilities agreement.

Placing a child for adoption

- Before a child can be placed for adoption, the agency must

  - be satisfied that the placement is in the child's best interests, and (after arranging for her/him to be visited) that the prospective adopter's premises are suitable for the child's needs;

- obtain, so far as reasonably practicable, all the information required by Sch.1;

- obtain medical reports completed within the last 12 months on the prospective adopters and on the child (after arranging any necessary investigations or tests, unless already done);

- arrange for the prospective adopters to be interviewed;

- enquire of other relevant local authorities (where the child or prospective adopters live, or where their premises are) to confirm that placement and adoption would not be detrimental to the child's welfare; and

- prepare a report on the above matters for the panel or other agency [reg.18].

Sch.1 is divided into 3 parts: Part I – information about the child; Part II – information about the child's family; Part III – information about the prospective adopters.

Consent

■ Parents may consent to a child's placement for adoption by signing a certificate in the form prescribed by Schedules 4 or 7 and returning it to the agency within 28 days of receipt [reg.19].

■ In the event that a certificate is not returned within 28 days, a parent cannot be contacted, or written notice is received withdrawing consent:

- registered adoption services must take any steps they consider in the child's best interests and refer to the local authority where the child lives, and

- local authorities (including those receiving such a referral) must proceed as if consent were not forthcoming [reg.20].

Application for a permanence order

■ Unless an adoption order application has been made, a local authority agency considering adoption for a child who is not subject to a supervision requirement must make an application for a permanence order within 28 days of:

- a) receipt of the certificate indicating a parent does not consent to adoption or

- b) deciding to proceed as if consent is not forthcoming [reg.21(1)–(2) and (4)].

■ The application must include requests for parental rights and responsibilities and authority for the child to be adopted [reg.21(3)].

■ Where a child is subject to a supervision requirement, the agency is obliged to refer the case to the Principal Reporter, but cannot do so until a certificate confirming consent has been received from each parent, or reg.20 applies (i.e. 28 days have expired and there is no response from the parent/s). The referral must be made in the form prescribed by Sch.8 [reg.22].

■ There is an obligation to make the referral to the Principal Reporter within 7 days where reg.20 applies [reg.23(1)–(2)].

■ Unless an adoption application has already been made:

- if the Children's Hearing report supports its decision, the agency must apply for a permanence order within 28 days from date of receipt of report, and the application must include requests for parental rights and responsibilities and authority for the child to be adopted;

- if the Children's Hearing report does not support its decision, the agency must review its decision within 28 days of receiving the report, taking account of the report and any other recommendations it may wish to seek, and notify the Principal Reporter of its decision [reg.23(3)–(8)]. If it decides adoption remains in the best interests of the child, the agency must apply for a permanence order within 28 days of the date of the Children's Hearing.

Notice of proposed application for a permanence order

■ A local authority proposing or required to apply for a permanence order and obliged to give notice under s.105 must supply the following prescribed information to the child's father (not married to the mother and without PRRs, and whose identity and whereabouts are known or can be obtained):

- the intended date and court of application;

- if the application will include authority for the child to be adopted;

- any intended ancillary provisions to be sought under s.82 [reg.23A].

Notice of proposed application for an adoption order

■ A local authority obliged to give notice under s.105 of an adoption order application must supply the following prescribed information to the child's father (not married to the mother and without PRRs, and whose identity and whereabouts are known or can be obtained):

- the court to which application has been or will be made, and

- the date of the preliminary hearing (where the application has been made), or

- the date on which the prospective adopters intend to apply (if known) [reg.25A].

Placement for adoption

■ Having decided that a prospective adopter is suitable to adopt and suitable for a particular child (i.e. following the formal match), the agency must provide the prospective adopter with full information about the child, including written information about the child's background, parentage, health and mental and emotional development, including the medical report on the child obtained under regulation 18. The agency must also provide written advice about telling a child about their adoption and origin, adopted people's rights to obtain information from the Registrar General, and counselling in that regard, and the availability of adoption support services [reg.24(1)–(2)].

- The agency must also provide notification of the adoption placement in writing to the Health Board for the area where the adopter lives, the local authority for that area (if not the agency) and the education authority if the child is of school age. If the medical adviser considers the child to have a problem of medical significance, the health board and education authority must be notified before placement. A report on the child's health and medical history must be sent to the prospective adopter's doctor before placement, with details of the proposed placement [reg.24(3)–(4) and (6)].

- Agencies must notify the child's parent/s, any parent/s without parental responsibility whose whereabouts are known (if considered in the child's best interests) and the child's guardian (if whereabouts known) when a child has been placed for adoption [reg.24(5)].

- After a child is placed for adoption and until an adoption order is made, the agency must ensure the child is visited and a written report placed on the case record within one week of placement and thereafter as often as the agency considers necessary for the child's well-being [reg.25].

Review of children not placed within 6 months of a permanence order with authority to adopt

- If a child has not been placed for adoption within 6 months of a permanence order with authority to adopt being granted, the agency must review the case as soon as practicable and then every 6 months until the child is placed [reg.26(1)–(2)].

- When reviewing a case under this regulation, agencies must:

  • consult and take account of the child's views (depending on age and maturity) and those of anyone with parental rights or responsibilities, and

  • assess the child's immediate and long-term needs, the reasons why no placement has been made, and any action necessary for the child's welfare [reg.26(3)].

- Agencies must record the findings of the review in writing and place this report on the child's file [reg.26(4)].

Case records: information to be kept about adoptions

- An agency must set up a case record for each prospective adopter and any child for whom a panel has recommended adoption, and place on it the information it has gathered, and the reports, recommendations and decisions of the agency or any panel [reg.27(1)–(2)].

- Agencies must continue to keep records set up under the 1996 Regulations.

- However, agencies are not required to keep information they have gathered if it would be prejudicial to an adopted person's welfare or if it is not reasonably practicable to keep it [reg.27(3)–(4)].

- Subject to the Adoption (Disclosure of Information & Medical Information about Natural Parents) (Scotland) Regulations 2009, case records must be treated as confidential. Records and indexes must be kept accessibly and securely and safeguarded from theft, unauthorised disclosure, damage, loss and destruction [reg.28(1)–(2)].

- Records and indexes may be kept on computer or such other system as reproduces the total contents, and must be retained:

  • in cases where an adoption order was made, for at least 100 years;

  • for prospective adopters where no order was made, for 10 years; and

  • in other cases, for as long as the agency considers appropriate [reg.28(3)–(4)].

The Adoption (Disclosure of Information & Medical Information about Natural Parents) (Scotland) Regulations 2009 [relating to ss.38, 74 and 117]

- The Adoption (Disclosure of Information & Medical Information about Natural Parents) (Scotland) Regulations provide for the disclosure of information about adoptions and about the health of natural parents of children who are to be or have been adopted, and came into force on 28 September 2009.

Disclosure of information about adoptions

- Regulations 3 and 4 apply when an adopted person seeks counselling under s.9 or information under ss.60–62 of the Act.

- Regulation 3 requires disclosure of adoption information held by an agency to an adopted person who is aged 16 or over in Scotland or aged 18 or over if in England or Wales [reg.3(1)].

- Information may also be disclosed to adoptees under 16 (18 in England and Wales) if the agency deems it appropriate; in deciding if it is appropriate, the agency must take into account the adoptee's views (according to age and maturity) and welfare, and the views of the adopters, if practicable. However, information capable of identifying natural parents or relatives must not be disclosed to under-age persons [reg.3(2)–(4)].

- When disclosing information under this regulation, agencies must inform the adopted person about counselling services [reg.3(5)].

- Reg.4 allows agencies to disclose adoption information to the local authority in England or Wales where the adoptee lives or the where the court made the adoption order if the person has sought information, to the Registrar General for England and Wales, or to the adoptee's local authority (or to the local authority where the court made the adoption order) in Scotland provided the person has applied for support services.

- Agencies may also allow access to and disclose information from adoption records to individuals in order to carry out their agency functions and to researchers with written authority from Scottish Ministers [reg.5].

- Agencies must allow access to and disclose information from adoption records to official inquiries, Scottish Ministers, the Scottish Public Services Ombudsman, the Scottish Commission for the Regulation of Care, anyone authorised under the Adoption Agencies (Scotland) Regulations 2009 and courts or officers appointed by them [reg.6].

- A record must be kept of any disclosure under regs.5 or 6 including reasons and the applicable regulation and paragraph [reg.7].

- Agencies must transfer case records in whole or part to another agency if it is in the interests of the adoptee/adopter to whom the record relates, and must keep a record of the transfer [reg.8(1)].

- When a registered adoption service ceases to exist or act as an adoption agency, it must transfer its records to:

  - a) another registered adoption service (subject to ministerial approval, and the receiving agency must notify in writing ministers and the adoptee/adopter to whom the record relates when the transfer has taken place);

  - b) the local authority for the area of its head office; or

  - c) the new agency in the case of a merger [reg.8(2)–(3)].

Disclosure of medical information about natural parents
- Reg.9 makes it clear that Part 3 of the regulations (relating to the disclosure of medical information about natural parents) are secondary to the Adoption Agencies (Scotland) Regulations 2009, and part 2 of these regulations (disclosure of information about adoptions), so that adoption agencies must make efforts to collect the required medical information in the normal way before having recourse to these regulations.

- Under reg.10, there is no automatic right for the child or her/his adoptive parent(s) to access any information collected under these regulations.

- Reg.11(1) requires a medical practitioner to disclose relevant information held on a child's family to an adoption agency on request. The relevant information is any history of genetically transmissible or other significant disease in either parent's family [Adoption Agencies (Scotland) Regulations 2009, Sch.1, Part III, Paragraph 13].

- Any information disclosed to an agency under reg.11 must be placed on the child's case record and treated as confidential [reg.11(2) and (3)].

The Adoption Support Services and Allowances (Scotland) Regulations 2009

- The Adoption Support Services and Allowances (Scotland) Regulations cover the provision of adoption support services by local authorities and the payment of allowances by adoption agencies, and came into force on 28 September 2009.

Notices to children
- Reg.3 requires that notices to be given to a child under 12, or to a child over 12 who is not of sufficient age or understanding in the local authority's opinion, must be given to the adopter or other appropriate adult.

Adoption support services
- Reg.4 requires local authorities to provide support for 3 years following the adoption order to a child they have placed for adoption outside their area and to:

  - the child's natural parents;

  - the child's adoptive parents;

- other children in the adoptive family [reg.4(1)–(2)(a)].

■ The support can be ended earlier than 3 years if the adopted child attains the age of 18, or if the person receiving the support, the local authority for the area where the person lives and the assessing local authority all agree [reg.4(2)(a) and (b)].

■ Local authorities may provide adoption support services to persons outside their area if they consider it appropriate to do so [reg.4(3)].

Assessments

■ Reg.5 allows local authorities to assess or reassess (under ss.9(1) or 49(2) respectively) the need for support services in relation to a specific service only, where the request relates to that service or the authority believes it is sufficient to do so [reg.5(1) and (3)].

■ Local authorities must start an assessment or reassessment of adoption support needs as soon as possible and no later than 4 weeks after:

- a request from a person under s.9(1)

- notice of a requirement from a relevant member under s.49(2) of the Act [reg.5(2) and (4)].

■ Assessments and reassessments must consider any of the following which are relevant:

- the person's needs and how they might be met;

- the adoptive family's needs and how they might be met;

- child's developmental and other needs and how they might be met;

- the adopter's parenting capacity;

- family and environment;

- circumstances leading to placement for adoption;

- any previous assessments of the person's support needs [reg.6(1) and 7(1)].

- The local authority carrying out an assessment or reassessment must:

  - if appropriate, interview the subject of any assessment, and if a child, also interview the adopter/s;

  - if a health service appears to be needed, consult the Health Board;

  - seek any other appropriate advice and information;

  - write a report of the assessment [reg.6(2) and 7(2)].

Notices
- People must be allowed to make representations before a decision about support service provision is made [reg.8(1)].

- Local authorities must give notice of the proposed decision and the time for making representations, which must be at least 2 weeks; the notice must include:

  - a statement of the person's support needs;

  - the basis for determining any financial support and the amount payable (if the decision relates to an adoption allowance);

  - the proposed support services (if any);

  - any conditions to be imposed under regulation 15 [reg.8(2) and (3)].

- If services are to be provided and an adoption support plan is required, a draft plan must accompany the notice [reg.8(4)].

- No decision can be made until the:

  - person has made representations or accepted the proposal and any draft plan, or

  - time limit for representations has expired [reg.8(5)].

■ When the local authority has made a decision about providing support services, it must notify the person, with reasons, and if an adoption support plan is required, it must accompany the notice [reg.9(1)–(2)].

■ For an adoption allowance the notice must state:

• how the amount is calculated;

• the amount, frequency, period and start date of payments by instalments or the date of any one-off payment;

• any conditions attached, any date by which they are to be met and what happens if they are not met;

• review, variation and termination procedures;

• the local authority's and adopter's respective responsibilities with regard to payment and reviews [reg.9(3)].

Adoption allowances – conditions for payment
■ Reg.10 provides for the payment of an adoption allowance to support or continue an adoption placement, provided that

• it is necessary to ensure the child can be looked after by the adoptive parent [reg.10(2)(a)];

• the child needs special care which requires greater resources because of illness, disability, emotional or behavioural difficulties or the effects of abuse or neglect [reg.10(2)(b)];

• special arrangements are necessary because of age or ethnic origin or to enable a child to be placed with a sibling or another child s/he has lived with [reg.10(2)(c)];

• it is to meet regular travel costs for contact [reg.10(2)(d)];

• as a contribution to adoption legal costs (including court fees), introductions or setting up costs, including furniture and equipment; adaptations to the home; transport; clothing, toys or other necessary items [reg.10(2)(e)].

Adoption allowances – payment of a reward element

- The adoption allowance may only include a reward element if the decision is made before the adoption order is made and the:

  - adopter was the child's foster carer or kinship carer, and

  - the fostering or kinship allowance included a reward element [reg.11(1)].

- The reward element is payable for 2 years from adoption (unless the agency considers it necessary for a child's exceptional needs or in other exceptional circumstances) [reg.11(2)].

Adoption allowances – type of payment

- An adoption allowance may be paid periodically if it is to meet a need which is likely to give rise to recurring expenditure, otherwise it is to be paid by a single payment, or if the parties agree, by instalments [reg.12].

Adoption allowances – matters to be taken into account

- When carrying out an assessment of the need for an adoption allowance, agencies must take account of any grant, benefit, allowance or resource available to the person as an adopter, to work out the amount of the allowance [reg.13(1)–(2)].

- Unless reg.13(4) or (5) applies, agencies must also take account of the:

  - person's financial resources, including state benefits payable for the child;

  - person's reasonable outgoings and commitments (excluding the child);

  - child's financial needs [reg.13(3)].

- Agencies *must* disregard the considerations in reg.13(3) in relation to payment of reasonable legal costs associated with the adoption order application, and in relation to payment of costs associated with introductions [reg.13(4)].

■ Agencies *may* disregard the considerations in reg.13(3) for:

- initial costs of accommodating the child;

- ongoing travel costs for contact purposes;

- any allowance payable under reg.10(2)(b) or (c);

- any reward element payable under reg.11 [reg.13(5)].

Adoption allowances – termination of payments

■ Adoption allowances stop when:

- the child no longer lives with the adopter/s (unless the agency considers the child's needs or exceptional circumstances require continued payment) [reg.14(a)];

- the child leaves full-time education or training and starts work;

- the child qualifies for income support or jobseeker's allowance;

- the child reaches 18, unless continuing in full-time education, when it may continue until the end of that course;

- any agreed period expires [reg.14].

Adoption allowances – conditions for payment

■ In order to receive periodic payments of an adoption allowance, adopters (both if a couple) must agree to:

- notify the local authority as soon as reasonably practicable (and if orally, confirm in writing in 7 days) of any new address, the child's death, any changes listed in reg.14 and any change in financial circumstances or the financial needs or resources of the child;

- supply an annual statement of financial circumstances and the financial needs and resources of the child, plus confirmation of address and that the child is still there [reg.15(1)].

■ Agencies may specify how and when allowances are to be used [reg.15(2)].

- Payments may be varied, suspended or stopped if any conditions are not met, and the agency may seek repayment of part or all of the amount paid; however, in the case of failure to supply an annual statement, the agency must first send a reminder giving 28 days to comply [reg.15(3) and (4)].

Review of adoption allowances

- Reg.16 requires agencies to review financial support on receipt of the annual statement; and if any circumstances change or any condition is breached as set out in reg.15; and at any other time appropriate to the adoption support plan [reg.16(1)–(3)].

- Adopters must be given the chance to make representations before a decision to reduce or stop payments or revise the plan, having first been notified of the proposed decision and the time allowed for making representations. The notice must contain the information listed in reg.8(3) and any revised draft plan. However, payments may be suspended pending a decision [reg.16(4)–(6)].

- Agencies must make a decision about variation, termination or recovery of any payments made, based on the review and any representations; they must then notify the person, with reasons [reg.16(7) and (8)].

Savings provision

- Allowances payable under 1996 regulations may continue to be paid, or the recipient may agree to receive instead an allowance under these regulations [reg.17].

Neither the miscellaneous provisions of Chapter 3 nor Schedule 1 (specified offences) and Schedule 2 (the certificate of eligibility and approval) have been included in this guide.

Source material

Primary legislation
- Adoption and Children (Scotland) Act 2007

- Children (Scotland) Act 1995

Subordinate legislation
- Adoption Agencies (Scotland) Regulations 2009

- Adoption Agencies (Scotland) Amendment Regulations 2010

- Adoption (Disclosure of Information and Medical information about Natural Parents) (Scotland) Regulations 2009

- Adoption Support Services and Allowances Regulations 2009

- Adoption and Children (Scotland) Act 2007 (Commencement No. 4, Transitional and Savings Provisions) Order 2009

Subject index